Table of Contents

A Word to the Reader 1

God Has Spoken 3

Personal Declarations 4

GOD'S GIFT OF FORGIVENESS 6

Day 1: Forgiveness Is a Gift from God 7

Day 2: God Is Faithful and Will Forgive 9

Day 3: Forgiveness Is a Blessing 11

Day 4: Your Transgressions Are Far Removed From You 14

Day 5: Everyone Who Believes Receives Forgiveness 17

Day 6: Your Sins Are Blotted Out and Forgotten 19

Day 7: God Is Merciful and Forgiving 21

POSITION YOUR HEART TO FORGIVE 23

Day 8: Love Covers Offense 24

Day 9: Love Always Protects 26

Day 10: A Heart Void of Iniquity 29

Day 11: Who Is Without Sin? 31

Day 12: We Are All Members of One Body 33

Day 13: Unforgiveness Hides the Face of God 36

Day 14: No Root of Bitterness 38

Day 15: Hatred Stirs Up Conflict 41

YOUR DUTY TO FORGIVE 44

Day 16: How Much Do You Love Him? 45

Day 17: Restore Your Offender 47

Day 18 A Gentle Versus A Harsh Word 49

Day 19: Even Sinners Love Those Who Love Them 51

Day 20: Confess To and Pray for One Another 54

Day 21: Privately Point Out Their Fault 57

Day 22: Repay Evil With Blessing 60

Day 23: Leave Your Gift On The Altar 63

Day 24: Living Peacefully with Others Depends on You 65

DO AS GOD DID AND CONTINUES TO DO, FORGIVE 68

Day 25: Forgive As The Lord Has Forgiven You 69

Day 26: Forgive As You Were Forgiven 72

Day 27: Forgive So That You May Be Forgiven 75

Day 28: Forgiveness Is Conditional 78

Day 29: Forgive and Be Forgiven 81

Day 30: Reaffirm Your Love By Forgiving 84

HELP FOR YOU TO FORGIVE 87

Day 31: You Need Faith to Forgive 88

Day 32: Be Ye Cleansed of All Filthiness of The Spirit 91

Day 33: Love One Another 93

Day 34: Seek Peace and Pursue It 96

Day 35: Slow Is Not Bad 98

YOU CAN FORGIVE..101

Day 36: Forgiveness Demonstrated 102

Day 37: The Antidote for Unforgiveness..105

Day 38: Love The Lord With Your All 107

Day 39: You Can Do It...110

Day 40: Abide In Him 113

Forgiveness Declarations 116

Sources 118

About the Author 120

Other Books by the Author...122

Follow Me to Stay Connected 127

The Spoken Word on Forgiveness.

A 40-Day Devotional

Rosemarie Downer, Ph.D.

The Spoken Word on Forgiveness

A 40-Day Devotional

by

Rosemarie Downer, Ph.D.

Copyright © 2022

ISBN: 979-8-9875327-6-8

Independently Published

First Edition

Scripture quotations marked (KJV) are taken from the Holy Bible, King James Version, Cambridge, 1769. Used by permission. All rights reserved.

Scripture quotations marked (NIV) are taken from the Holy Bible, New International Version®, NIV®. Copyright © 1973, 1978, 1984 by Biblica, Inc.™ Used by permission of Zondervan. All rights reserved worldwide. www.zondervan.com

All rights reserved. No part of this publication may be reproduced or transmitted in any form or by any means, electronic or mechanical, including photocopy, recording, or any information storage retrieval system, without permission in writing from the copyright owner.

Dedication

This devotional is dedicated to all who desires to prosper and be in health even as their soul prospers (3 John 2). It is your Heavenly Father's desire that you are whole — healthy in your soul (your will, emotions, and thoughts), body, and spirit. My desire for you is no different.

I pray that as you read and meditate upon the Scriptures herein, you will be made whole and strengthened in your inner man.

A Word to the Reader

The Scriptures that are discussed in this devotional all pertain to the mandate given to us by our Heavenly Father to forgive. So why an entire devotional on forgiveness? This is necessary because forgiveness places a high demand on us; a demand that is beyond our ability to obey without the help of the Holy Spirit. Forgiveness contradicts the carnality of humankind; it is entirely opposite to our sensual nature. It is the extreme opposite of what we, when operating in the flesh, want to do. So, we desperately need the help of the Holy Spirit to obey this mandate.

To obtain help from the Holy Spirit — our Paraclete, Teacher, Guide, and Comforter — we must hear with our hearts what the Father has said about forgiveness. By hearing what the Father has said, we come in alignment with this mandate. So, what better place to go to than the written / spoken Word of God to obtain the help we need and to hear what thus saith the Lord?

I advise you my beloved brother, sister, and friend to meditate upon the Scriptures as you read each one. Read one daily reading per day, and if you need more time to think upon any day's reading, do not move on to the next reading until that Word is settled in your spirit. If you are still meditating or pondering a verse or a day's reading, do not move on to the next day's reading until you have settled that verse in your spirit. Read *and* marinate in the words. The idea is not to read the devotional in one sitting or to read it as fast as you can. The idea is to read and absorb what you read into your person — into your spirit — so that you can be transformed.

I suggest you look up and read all the Scriptures discussed in at least two Bible versions that are different from the versions used. I also suggest you read further about the Scriptures in at least one Bible commentary so that you can get a deeper understanding of what each verse is saying. I'm advising you meditate upon each verse; that is, after getting a clear understanding of each verse, apply the Word to your personal situation so that you can improve your ways. Think about how each Scripture can be meaningful to you. Think about what changes you need to make to obey each verse. Be specific in asking the Lord to help you make the necessary changes. The objective of this devotional is that you become more like Christ, especially in your interpersonal relationships. Therefore, as you read, you must think and pray about transformation through and by the Word.

Also, as you meditate upon the verses, do so to the point where you can then communicate what each verse is saying to you and to someone else in your own words. When you can do that, you know that the verse has seeped beneath the surface (your intellect) and have gotten down into your spirit. This is the goal because without the Word of God getting in your spirit, you will not be transformed.

Psalm 119:130 tells us that the entrance of His Word gives us light, and they are healing to all our flesh. So, my beloved reader, let the Word of God heal you. *"All our flesh"* means it will heal your body, your soul, and your spirit. Your soul contains what you think, what you feel which is your emotions, and what you desire which is your will. So, the Word of God will heal your body, they will heal your spirit, and they will heal your thoughts, your feelings, and your desire. Get your healing!

You are about to embark on a 40-day journey that is loaded with Scriptures. This journey will remind you about the love of your Heavenly Father who so graciously forgives you and that you should in turn give that gift of forgiveness to those who hurt you. Also, you will be reminded that help to forgive your offender is readily available to you. If you open your spirit to receive what thus saith the Lord, I promise, you will be transformed. You cannot have an encounter with the Lord Jesus Christ and remain the same.

[24] *The Lord bless you and keep you;* [25] *the Lord make his face shine on you and be gracious to you;* [26] *the Lord turn his face toward you and give you peace.*

(Numbers 6:24-26, NIV)

God Has Spoken

The Word of God is a lamp to our feet and a light to our path (Psalm 119:105). The Word of God shows us where to put our feet and they shed light on the path ahead of us so that we will know the direction to go.

Without God's Word, we will find ourselves floundering around in the dark, going down the wrong paths, tripping over obstacles, and falling into traps that are set by the enemy of our souls. Without the Word of God guiding us, we would lose our way in life; our lives would be in ruins.

The Word of God helps us understand what God wants from us as Christians and teaches us how to live a life that pleases God and that gives Him glory. God hates sin and wants us to hate it as well. The Word of God is what gives us the strength and guidance we need to resist sin — the besetting sins in our lives and the things that so easily entangle us.

God has spoken on the issue of forgiveness, and God's Word bring blessings. God's spoken Word on forgiveness will sustain you through pain, will purify you so that unforgiveness and bitterness will not take root in you, will comfort, and strengthen you, and will foster spiritual growth.

God's Word bring the assurance that forgiveness is a gift from the Father to us, that we should forgive as He has forgiven us, and that we cannot forgive in our own strength. Also, the Word reminds us that the consequences of unforgiveness are grave and that forgiveness is not negotiable.

God has spoken on forgiveness so that you may have life. He has spoken to revive the places in your life that hurt and offense have killed. God has spoken to equip you for every good work, including forgiving your offender.

God has spoken on forgiveness, listen and take heed!

Personal Declarations

Repeat these confessions aloud to yourself until you believe them. You can structure your prayers around them as well as journal about them if you like to write.

1. God's Word is the power that I need to transform my life.
2. My heart, soul, and spirit are open to hear the Word of God.
3. As the Word of God enters my spirit, I shall receive life.
4. As the Word of God enters my spirit, I shall become more like Christ.
5. As the Word of God enters my spirit, I shall lay aside every weight and the sins that easily beset and entangle me. (Hebrews 12:1)
6. The Word of God is life to me and health to all my flesh. (Proverbs 4:22)
7. I open my spirit for the Word of God to penetrate my soul and to judge the thoughts and attitudes of my heart. (Hebrews 4:12)
8. Lord, I will hear Your Word. I will hear what You have said about forgiveness, and I will put them into practice. (James 1:22)
9. Lord I will take heed to Your Word so that rivers of living water will flow from within me. (John 7:38)
10. I am sanctified because I accept Your Word oh Lord. (John 17:17)
11. Lord, I have hidden Your Word in my heart so that I might not sin against You. (Psalm 119:11)
12. I know the truth of Your Word Lord, and it will set me free. (John 8:22)
13. Your Word is perfect, and it shall revive my soul. (Psalm 19:7)
14. I am attentive to Your Word; I incline my ears to Your sayings. (Proverbs 4:20)
15. Your Word will not escape from my sight; I will keep them in my heart. (Proverbs 4:21)

16. The eyes of my heart are open, and I will behold wondrous things in Your Word. (Psalm 110:18)
17. I am clothed in the Word of God and am an imitator of God. (Ephesians 5:1)
18. I have great peace, and nothing shall offend or stumble me because I love Your Word. (Psalm 119:165)
19. God, Your Word has revived me and given me life. (Psalm 119:50)
20. I have received divine revelation from God my Father. I have a deep understanding of what I read in Your Word.

GOD'S GIFT OF FORGIVENESS

Day 1: Forgiveness Is a Gift from God

In Him we have redemption through His blood, the forgiveness of our trespasses, according

to the riches of His grace.

—*Ephesians 1:7 (KJV)*

A gift is not something we earn, nor is it anything for which we must pay a price. A gift is usually given to someone without that person asking for it. It is something that is given of a free will by the giver. Sometimes a gift is a surprise to the recipient. The recipient gets this wonderful thing surprisingly and is not expected to do or pay anything in return. In some cases, when given a gift, we do not feel like we deserve it. Therefore, a gift is a blessing; it is a good thing, an endowment, a donation, a bequest that is pronounced upon us, often unexpectedly and often beyond our expectations.

The greatest gift given was made by our Heavenly Father to us, fallen man. That gift is forgiveness of our trespasses and sins. He gave us this gift out of the unending riches of His glory. Through the blood of Jesus Christ our Savior, God's only Son, we have redemption. That is the greatest gift.

Our Heavenly Father loves us far beyond the love anyone in this world could possibly have for us. He loves us unconditionally. There is absolutely nothing we could do to make Him love us any less or any more than He does.

How did God make this gift known to us? How did He convey this gift to us? He saw us in sin and degradation before we even knew we needed a savior. He planned for our redemption before the foundation of the world. He ordained for us to be in relationship with Him, so He redeemed us through the blood of His dear Son, Jesus.

God sent His only Son from heaven into this dark evil world to take on the form of man and walk the road to Calvary. There He laid down His life and shed His blood for our redemption. This is the gift of God. It was given for you so that today you may be forgiven of your sins and have access to the throne of grace in prayer, fellowship, and relationship with God your Father. This gift is so freely given that when you come before the Great High Priest, the King of Kings, the Lord of Lords, He stretches forth His scepter to you to let you know that you are welcomed in His presence.

What a great gift! And yes, you do not have to pay Him back for it. It is a gift that you did not ask for and that you do not deserve, but it is yours.

There is no greater blessing that God could have given to you than the precious life of His only begotten Son, so that in Him you may be redeemed from death and hell and receive forgiveness of sins and everlasting life.

Your Response

Pray that you live your life in a manner that glorifies God. **Give thanks** to your Heavenly Father for His amazing gift of salvation and **pray** that many who have not accepted Jesus as their Savior will do so before it is too late.

Day 2: God Is Faithful and Will Forgive

If we confess our sins, he is faithful and just and will forgive us our sins and purify us from all unrighteousness.

—*1 John 1:9 (NIV)*

What peace and comfort we get from knowing that if we sin, we can go to God our Father, confess our sins to Him, and be forgiven. There is no condition on this offer. There is no indication that this offer is good for some sins and not others. In fact, He assures us that He is *"faithful and just and will forgive us our sins and purify us from <u>all</u> unrighteousness."* (1 John 1:9, emphasis added).

According to Scriptures (Leviticus 5:5; 16:21; Numbers 5:7; Ezra 10:1), confession of sins has always been seen as a godly practice among those who turn to the Lord and as a source of healing (James 5:16). God assures us in His Word that He will forgive and remove our sins when we confess our sins to Him. So, although Believers are forgiven at the point of salvation, we must maintain a contrite heart before God. We must know that though we are not sinners, we are not sinless. Therefore, we must confess our sins to obtain forgiveness and cleansing from God.

When we have a disagreement with anyone, it creates a breach in fellowship with that individual and it creates a barrier between us and God. When arguments occur between us and another, it does not matter who is wrong. If there is a breach in fellowship, both parties are responsible. This is where the confession of sins become important. The goal is to maintain unity in the Spirit in the bond of peace (Ephesians 4:3), and that is everyone's responsibility. So, whether you caused or behaved unseemly during the argument, because the unity of the Spirit is broken, you must assume responsibility. And the appropriate response here is to confess to the faithful One so that He can cleanse, forgive, and restore.

Perhaps you were the victim of abuse, slander, disrespect, fraud, or a different type of violation. So, you may be wondering what you should confess if you are the victim, why you should confess, why you should be responsible in any way for the breach in relationship. But because you are told in Scriptures to seek peace and pursue it (Psalm 34:14) and do all you can to live peaceably with everyone (Romans 12:18), you must assume some responsibility and do what you can to repair the breach. You can pray about the situation, you can pray for your offender, specifically, you can pray that your offender be convicted and come to God in repentance. Having received Christ by faith, we have been forgiven of all our trespasses (Colossians 2:13). But although we are forgiven of all our trespasses, we see in 1 John 1:9 that God provides ongoing help for those who are already forgiven of all their sins because redeemed from sin or not, we are all susceptible to sin. This is good news! Jesus paid full price for our sins on the cross, so there is no remaining sin to be forgiven, but the throne room is open to us for ongoing forgiveness. Therefore, Christ is now seated at the right hand of God the Father, making intercession for us (Romans 8:34). Christ lives to secure the forgiveness of all our trespasses, now and forever.

1 John 1:9 is an acknowledgement of our ongoing need for help and a reassurance of the work of Christ for us. Forgiveness is a definite effect based on Jesus' work on the cross and it is a blessing, a gift to you and me.

Your Response

Do you experience a sense of guilt that you are never doing enough to please God? Is there a lingering fear that maybe God does not love or accept you? Do you ever feel like you have made the same mistakes enough times and so, you cannot go back to God for forgiveness of those sins? **Read** 1 John 1:9 over and over. **Read** it in various versions of the Bible. **Tell** yourself and **accept** the fact that your relationship with God is not based on performance, but instead, it is based on His unconditional love for you. **Thank** Him for His love for you and **pray** that you will in return love Him with all your heart.

Day 3:
Forgiveness Is a Blessing

¹ Blessed is the one whose transgressions are forgiven, whose sins are covered. ² Blessed is the one whose sin the Lord does not count against them and in whose spirit is no deceit.

—*Psalm 32:1-2 (NIV)*

What is a blessing and from whom do blessings come? A blessing is a favor, good wishes or approval, benefit, goodness, answer to prayer, or a gift from God. Therefore, the source of blessings is God our Father. What is favor? Favor is unprecedented kindness. It is compassion in which God puts Himself in our place and take the consequences while shielding us from them. Another word we can include as we discuss blessing is grace. Grace is often referred to as unmerited favor. In fact, the very meaning of grace is favor. Therefore, blessing is the grace or favor of God.

The forgiveness of our sins is a blessing — a gift, a favor — from God our Father. Sin deserves punishment. Sin is transgression of God's law; it is the defying of God's authority. But God in His unmatched love forgives our transgressions and covers our sins. He does not count our sins against us, and He cleanses our spirit of deceit. This is real forgiveness; it doesn't just quiet our conscience. It doesn't just abate guilt; it cancels the debt we owe the One against whom we transgress.

The forgiveness of your sins makes you a ransomed soul who now can have peace and rejoice in the wonders of the grace of your God. You must know that your sins are forgiven, and you must talk and act like you know this fact. As well, you must know that your sins are no longer exposed, they are covered by the love of Jesus Christ. Proverbs 16:6 (NIV, emphasis added) tells us that "*Through love and faithfulness sin is atoned for.*" The ultimate cause of the forgiveness and covering of your sins is the unending, unconditional, relentless love of God.

Blessed is the one whose transgressions are forgiven! According to Charles Spurgeon, this should give you reason for "double joy, bundles of happiness, and mountainous delight." Psalm 32 shows one way to be blessed — to make full confession and repentance of sin — and Psalm 1 tells the way to be blessed. We must not walk in the counsel of the ungodly or stand in the path of sinners, but we must delight in God's Word. That is, we must love His Word, love what He tells us to do, and express that love through our actions. In other words, we are blessed if we obey God's Word.

David, a great man of God had the opportunity to know this blessedness in his own life. God Himself referred to David as man after His heart, but David had some significant bouts of sin. Prominent among these were David's time at Ziklag (1 Samuel 27, 29, 30) and David's sin regarding Bathsheba and Uriah (2 Samuel 11), but David confessed his sins, repented of them, and was forgiven by God. He was blessed. His sins were covered.

You too have sinned. In fact, we all have sinned. No one is sinless. But have you confessed? Have you repented? Is your conscience pierced so that you know what it is like to be convicted by your deeds? Do you know the seriousness of sin? Do you know how good it is to be truly forgiven by God? *Blessed* is he whose transgression is forgiven, whose sin is covered. According to Trapp, "Sin is an odious thing, the devil's drivel or vomit, the corruption of a dead soul, the filthiness of flesh and spirit." Confess your sins to Him today, repent and turn from them, and enjoy the blessings of the God who loves you more than words can tell.

Your Response

Thank the Lord for His love towards you, a love that is sufficient to forgive you of any sin, any transgression against Him. **Take advantage** of the opportunity to be cleansed of all filthiness of your flesh and of your spirit. **Confess** your faults to Him. **Know** that it is His grace and mercy that is sustaining you from day to day, and that His desire is to fellowship with you, but you must first be forgiven of your transgressions.

Day 4:
Your Transgressions Are Far Removed From You

¹¹ *For as high as the heavens are above the earth, so great is his love for those who fear him;* ¹² *as far as the east is from the west, so far has he removed our transgressions from us.*

—Psalm 103:11-12 (NIV)

Whatever God does is done to the fullest, it is always done well, and that includes the forgiveness of your sins. When God forgives your sins, despite how you feel, and despite what others may think or say, you are forgiven. When God forgives, He removes your transgressions far from you. That means you no longer carry them; they are no longer associated with you. They are taken away. Psalm 103:12 says, *"as far as the east is from the west, so far has he removed our transgressions from us."*

In Psalm 103:11, David describes God's unfailing love for those who reverence Him: *"For as high as the heavens are above the earth, so great is his love for those who fear him."* The word fear here is not referring to terror, dread, or fright. It means adoration, worship, reverence, standing in awe of. If we recognize the greatness of God, that God, not us and not another is God, we will revere Him.

God's love is so great that the best way David could describe it was to compare it with the distance between the heavens above and the earth beneath. Just by looking up, David knew there was tremendous distance from the earth to the heavens. He recognized the heavens as extremely distant from the earth and he knew God's love for him, and His people stretched beyond that. David probably used this analogy because as a shepherd, he spent a lot of time gazing at the heavens and marveling at God's creative power (Psalm 8:3-4; 19:1).

THE SPOKEN WORD ON FORGIVENESS. A 40-DAY DEVOTIONAL

David spent a great deal of his life in the open fields as a shepherd caring for his father's sheep and later in the outdoors as a fugitive from the well-known jealous and insecure Saul. So, he knew from observation that there was great distance between the two.

The best demonstration of God's love for us is the death of Christ on the cross. John 3:16 tells us that God's love, being so potent, so compelling, and so powerful, God gave His only Son to pay the price for the sins of humankind and that act of love is not where it ends. *"He who did not spare his own Son, but gave him up for us all—how will he not also, along with him, graciously give us all things?"* (Romans 8:32, NIV, emphasis added). *"Christ Jesus who died and rose from the — more than that, who was raised to life — is at the right hand of God and is also interceding for us"* (Romans 8:34b, NIV, emphasis added). God loves us so much that no power on earth can destroy it.

What's alluded to in verse 12 — *"as far as the east is from the west, so far has he removed our transgressions from us"* — is no less significant than the reference drawn in verse 11. No one can measure the distance between the east and the west, not even in light years, and there is no end to the east or the west. The east and west has never met and will never meet. They are opposite directions from each other. Therefore, when God forgives you, your sins are in the opposite direction from you, and if you, after being forgiven, move and continue to move in the direction of a forgiven state, you will never meet your sins again.

This is good news! God's steadfast love and forgiveness far exceed the weight of your sins. His steadfast love is higher than the heavens, let alone your sins. Jesus is the means of your redemption.

Your Response

Show your reverence for the Lord by **worshipping** Him, and **verbally expressing** your gratitude to Him for His unending love towards you. **Ask** Him for grace to aid you in loving Him by obeying His Word. **Read** John 14:15 and meditate on it. **Pray** that all tendencies to hold on to sin and guilt even after God has forgiven you will be removed. **Pray** that the words of man or their actions toward you will no longer cause you to stumble, but instead, you will stand firm in God and will let nothing move you.

Day 5:
Everyone Who Believes Receives Forgiveness

All the prophets testify about him that everyone who believes in him receives forgiveness

of sins through his name.

—Acts 10:43 (NIV)

Peter was in Caesarea Maritima, the Roman capital of Samaria and Judea, at the home of Cornelius, a Roman centurion who devoutly followed Yahweh. An angel appeared to Cornelius and told him to send for Peter. Meanwhile, Peter received a vision that meant God's saving grace has no discrimination between Jews and Gentiles, but Peter thought at first that the vision was referring to clean and unclean meats. Peter went with the messengers that Cornelius sent and upon arrival at Cornelius' house, found a household of people ready to hear his testimony of Jesus (Acts 10:1–33). These people believed in Jesus and were ready to receive forgiveness of sins through His name.

"Forgiveness" is from the Greek root word aphesis. The word aphesis means a victim voluntarily relinquish their right to personally punish or avenge their aggressor. This does not mean the perpetrator goes unpunished. The governing authorities will still hold the perpetrator legally and financially responsible for their crime, but the action in response to the infraction comes from the law, not the victim.

Similarly, we must give up what we think is our right to take revenge on our offenders and let the governing law, God our defender, judge the matter. Romans 12:19 (NIV) instructs us in this manner: "*Do not take revenge, my dear friends, but leave room for God's wrath, for it is written: "It is mine to avenge; I will repay," says the Lord*". An Old Testament Scripture that gives a similar advice is Exodus 14:14 (NIV): "*The Lord will fight for you; you need only to be still.*"

Whoever, including you, believes in Christ through faith shall receive the gift of God's grace, the free and full forgiveness of sins. This gift is not due to anything any man deserves because no man deserves the love of God; it is an act of God's grace and mercy toward us. Whoever believes in Christ as the Lord, Savior, and Redeemer of humankind, whoever embraces the truth that God's forgiveness of our sins is a function of His Spirit that works according to His love, shall receive the gift of forgiveness.

Forgiveness from God is free and is available to all. Money or our works of righteousness, not even our act of repentance can procure (or earn) our forgiveness. There is nothing that we the created beings can do to earn forgiveness from the Creator. The key word here is "procure," which means to obtain something, especially through works, or with care and effort. God wants us to repent. In fact, we are urged to repent and turn from our sins numerous times in the Scriptures (i.e., Matthew 4:17, Luke 24:47, and Isaiah 30:15). But our act of repentance is not what make God forgive us, it is His love for us that moves Him with compassion to forgive us. So, despite their circumstances, whoever looks by faith to God for forgiveness, shall be forgiven. That includes you.

Your Response

Take a few minutes to **give God thanks** for His gift of forgiveness. **Thank Him** for His love for you. **Ask** for forgiveness of your sins — sins of omission and sins of commission. **Repent** of anything you might have thought, said, or done that was displeasing to God. Remember that repentance is sincere regret or remorse, godly sorrow, and the cessation of the wrong deeds being done. Once you have prayed in faith, **accept** His gift of forgiveness.

Day 6:
Your Sins Are Blotted Out and Forgotten

I, even I, am he who blots out your transgressions, for my own sake, and remembers your sins no more.

—Isaiah 43:25 (NIV)

We all have sinned and continue to sin, but we have been redeemed and have been transitioned from the kingdom of darkness to the kingdom of light. Although we are redeemed from sin to grace, we are all prone to sin, but we no longer live a life of habitual sin. Therefore, we are not sinners because sinning is not our lifestyle, but neither are we sinless. Hence, we need God's forgiveness when we sin.

Think of the many times — saved or unsaved — you sinned. Now think of the sins you repeatedly commit; the many things you do that you do not want to do. The Apostle Paul in Romans 7:15-20 addresses this. This Scripture says that we do not understand what we do because we do not do what we want to do, but instead we do what we hate. This is why we weep before the Lord when we keep doing those things that we are trying so desperately to stop doing. We sin because we have two laws warring in our members, and because we sin, we need God's forgiveness.

But God is longsuffering, merciful, gentle, and loving toward us. His love is enduring. He never turns away anyone who comes to Him in faith. Psalm 51:17 (KJV) says, *"a broken and a contrite heart, O God, thou wilt not despise."* So, when we go to Him for forgiveness, He grants it and after forgiving our sins, He does not remember them. When He forgives, He *never* reminds us of our sins because He does not keep record of them. He blots them out.

Isaiah 43:25 was addressing the children of Israel, God's chosen people. You have been adopted into the fold and is now a child of God, so these words are now addressing you. Too often, you like the children of Israel have done evil in the sight of the Lord, and in His justice, God could have unleashed severe consequences for your sin, but despite His legitimate case against you, in His righteous wrath, He is always merciful.

Note that God not only blot out our sins because He loves us, but He also blots out our sins for His name's sake. His integrity is on the line, so, the combination of His unfathomable love for us and the upholding of His name secure our forgiveness of sins by the God of mercy and grace. It is for God's own sake and for the sake of His holy name that He will never break His promises to His children. Your God is a covenant-keeping God; all His promises are "yes" and "amen" in Him.

God is holy and God is righteous, and His Word never fails. Numbers 23:19 tells us that God is not human, and therefore, He cannot lie. He does whatever He says He is going to do, and He keeps His promises. You have the assurance that the intentions of the God you serve can never be shaken. The Words of the Lord are faithful and true, and they are a sure promise to a thousand generations (Deuteronomy 7:9). Therefore, in His grace and mercy you can rejoice over these words: *"I, even I, am he who blots out your transgressions, for my own sake, and remembers your sins no more."*

Your Response

Read Isaiah 43:25 and Numbers 23:19 in various versions of the Bible and **meditate** upon the character and nature of the God you serve. **Obtain** peace from knowing that your God is a promise keeper and that He simply cannot lie. **Tell** yourself that even if the devil reminds you of the sins for which God has already forgiven you, you will **override** that with the promise that God remembers your sins no more. And do not only tell yourself that, **act** accordingly.

Day 7: God Is Merciful and Forgiving

The Lord our God is merciful and forgiving, even though we have rebelled against him.

—Daniel 9:9 (NIV)

A general definition for mercy is the compassionate treatment of those in distress, especially when it is within one's power to punish or harm them. The word "mercy" derives from the medieval Latin word merced or merces, which means "price paid." Mercy implies forgiveness, kindness, and benevolence. In keeping with the Latin word merced or merces, mercy appears in the Bible in the context of forgiveness or the withholding of punishment. The leading example of mercy is God's sacrificial gifting of His Son, Christ Jesus, on the cross of Calvary to pay the price for our sins.

God is abundant in mercy, and not only that, but He is also compassionate and slow to anger (Psalm 103:8). He is ever so patient with us. The fountain of mercy is within Him, and the streams of compassion that flow from Him are numerous in number; it is called "*the multitude of his tender mercies*" (Psalm 51:1). All spiritual favors and blessings flow from Him, particularly the forgiveness of all sorts of sins and of all sorts of sinners. This is the Lord's expressed love for us. It is due to the tender mercies of our God, and the riches of His grace that He abundantly pardons all who come to Him, and forgives all trespasses (Psalms 130:4, Psalms 130:7) though we have rebelled against Him.

There is mercy and forgiveness with the Lord, even for the worst of us. All have, sinned against Him, be He has spared us and not destroyed us. If He did not have mercy on us and did not forgive our sins, we would perish in them, and there would be no hope of salvation for us.

The parable of the prodigal son (Luke 15:11-32) shows that the God you serve will forgive you even when you dishonor and rebel against everything He wants you to do. It is a reminder that, like the father did for the prodigal son, God will restore you even when you reach your lowest. You might have squandered your inheritance of being made in His image, but in grace and mercy your Heavenly Father is at this very moment speaking to you. He is saying "come on home my child, I never stopped loving you."

Your Response

Read Lamentations 3:22-23 in various versions of the Bible and **meditate** upon it. **Pray** a prayer of thanksgiving and give God thanks for His unending love and mercy toward you. **Thank** and **praise** God for His loving-kindness and great mercy which are new every morning and in which He preserves you and not consume you.

POSITION YOUR HEART TO FORGIVE

Day 8:
Love Covers Offense

Whoever would foster love covers over an offense, but whoever repeats the matter separates close friends.

—Proverbs 17:9 (NIV)

God has many attributes, including but not limited to holy, faithful, omniscient (all-knowing), omnipotent (all-powerful), omnipresent, omnibenevolent (supremely good), immutable, merciful, glorious, and wise. But one that I believe top them all is love. God is love; that is simply who He is. Everything about God says love, and He loves us infinitely. The love of God is eternal, sovereign, unchanging, and limitless. That is why He gives us brand new mercies every morning. That is why He is ever so compassionate toward us. That is why He is longsuffering, patient, and kind toward us when we sin, and when we come to Him with a broken and contrite heart. His love covers us like a blanket covers an orphan out in the cold. His love covers our sin. His love knows no beginning and no ending.

Because we are born of God, we must be like Him. Therefore, if God our Father loves, then we must love too. If we do not love, then we do not know God, because God is love (1 John 4:7-8). One of the innumerable ways that God shows His love for us is by forgiving us of our sins and remembering them no more. Here in Proverbs 17:9, He is asking the very same of you. He is asking you to love your neighbor, yes, the very neighbor that wronged you. He is asking you to love them enough to forgive them and don't keep record of the wrong they did. His Word requires that you forgive them and cover their wrong against you with your love for them, just like God does for you. God is asking you to love them more than you are hurt by what they did to you.

Proverbs 17:9 is calling you to walk in true love and friendship. The abiding love of God in you will make you pardon and stop thinking about personal offences against you. In the absence of the love of God in you, you will regurgitate the offenses done against you and that will hinder the growth of good relationships and destroy peaceful relationships. Also, with the love of God in you, you will never repeat a person's failures or sins to others, but void of the love of God, you will be found backbiting, talebearing, and whispering (Proverbs 10:12; 11:13; 16:28) against your offender.

Covering a wrong done against you is how you show love, and according to Scripture this is an effective means of winning friends. This kind deed silences every backbiting tongue and drives away every talebearer and whisperer (Proverbs 18:8; 20:19; 25:23; 26:20-22; Psalm 101:5). This kind of love will restrain you from slander — repeating rumors or facts that degrade a person's reputation.

You are called to walk in true love, the love of God. This love thinks no evil of others and does not rejoice when it hears of failures or sins in others' lives (I Corinthians 13:4-7). When you cover a person's transgression or wrong against you, you bury news that reflects poorly on the person's character. This kind of love protects the reputations of others.

Your Response

Make a list of as many Scriptures as you can that talk about the love of God. **Read** them over and over so that you can get a deeper understanding of the nature of God's love. Now, **ask** God to fill you with His love. Know that every attribute of God flows out of His number one characteristic – love. So, **pray** to be more like Christ, **pray** to be ruled by His love so that everything else about you will reflect the love of God.

Day 9:
Love Always Protects

^{4} Love is patient, love is kind. It does not envy, it does not boast, it is not proud. ^{5} It does not dishonor others, it is not self-seeking, it is not easily angered, it keeps no record of wrongs. ^{6} Love does not delight in evil but rejoices with the truth. ^{7} It always protects, always trusts, always hopes, always perseveres.

—*1 Corinthians 13:4-7 (NIV)*

Forgiveness is an act of love in many ways. Love through forgiveness was first demonstrated when the God of creation sent His only Son from heaven where there is no flaw or distress to earth, the place that is fraught with sin, pain, and loss. God gave His Son a ransom for us to bring us into relationship with Him because He loves us. Scriptures such as 1 John 4:8 and 16 and Romans 5:8 tell us that God is love. And the well-known Scripture John 3:16 (KJV) — *"For God so loved the world, that he gave his only begotten Son, that whosoever believeth in him should not perish, but have everlasting life"* — is a bold fact and very strong evidence of God's love for His children; that is, you and me.

Unforgiveness is the withholding of pardon for wrong done to an individual. On the contrary, forgiveness is the writing off or pardoning of a wrong done to a person. Therefore, in the case of forgiveness, instead of seeking retribution, the offended wipes the slate clean, presses the reset button, and proceeds with the understanding that the offender owes them nothing. One can only pardon a wrong that was done to them and move one without seeking retribution if they are acting out of the love of God. This love that fuels the offended to act in this manner covers and protects the offender.

The main contributor to unforgiveness is the absence of love. Put differently, instead of love, forgiveness is fueled by apathy, an uncaring and possibly hateful attitude. However, despite being dealt injustice, the offended is required by God to care for and love the offender. Thus, an indication of the lack God's love in an individual is their inability to forgive. This may sound unfair to the person who has been offended, because you may think that the person who caused the offense is the one who lacks love. While that is true, the offended is unable to forgive and sometimes even unable to accept a pardon from the offender because they also do not love.

My main reason for the above conclusion is that when we cannot forgive, we fail to realize God's love for us that rescued us from sin. If we have done so much that offends God and, despite that, He gave His only Son as our Redeemer, then we must forgive others. Unfortunately, that is often not the case. The primary reason for unforgiveness is we do not understand or appreciate the depth of the love God has toward us; therefore, though commanded by Scripture (John 15:12) to do so, we cannot love others as He loves us.

Forgiveness is an act of love, and it is unselfish. Like God Himself, He does not want you to love conditionally; He wants you to love blindly.

Forgiveness and other unselfish acts are good demonstrations of the love of Christ. Christ demonstrated His unconditional love for us through the ultimate act of unselfishness. His death on the cross secures our forgiveness of sins and it covers and protects us, and so will your forgiveness of your offender's wrongdoing against you.

Your love through forgiveness will demonstrate patience with your offender, it will show kindness, and it will be void of envy. Because of the abiding love of God in you, you will not dishonor or expose the wrongdoing of your offender; instead, you will protect them. Love always protects. This love will empower you to seek the interest of the offender not yourself, it will restrain you from becoming easily angered, and like God towards you, you will not keep record of the wrong that was done to you.

Your Response

Read 1 Corinthians 13:4-7 and **write down** the adjectives of love that are listed in the verses; for example, kind, not envious, not boastful (humble), honor others, etc. After listing them, **pray** into each one and as you pray, **acknowledge** before God that you need His help to forgive in accordance with His Word. Let Him know that you are fully aware that apart from the help of the Holy Spirit, you cannot and will not forgive, but you want to.

Day 10:
A Heart Void of Iniquity

If I regard iniquity in my heart,

the Lord will not hear me.

—Psalm 66:18 (NIV)

Undoubtedly, God is merciful and kind, but will He answer our prayers if there is sin in our hearts? There can be any number of reasons, such as doubt or lack of faith, impatience, and praying amiss for unanswered prayers, but sin might be the biggest reason our prayers are not answered. Psalm 66:18 is a verse I almost always reference when I teach on forgiveness, and the question I often ask is "Is it worth it?" Is it worth harboring unforgiveness and run the risk of praying prayers that God does not hear? Put bluntly, God will not answer our prayers if we willfully hold on to any evil way, unforgiveness included.

If we listen to the devil, God will not listen to us. If we refuse to hear God's commands, He will surely not hear our prayers. God would not be the holy God of truth and justice He said He is if He delights in our prayers and devotions while we are gratifying ourselves with sin.

Sadly, because of iniquity in the hearts of many Believers, too many pray but their prayers go unanswered. God's Word is clear that we have all sinned and have fallen short of His glory (Romans 3:23). Yes, we all sin, but we should not have un-confessed and un-repented sin in our life. We must confess our sins and repent as we are commanded in Acts 17:30 (NIV): "*In the past God overlooked such ignorance, but now he commands all people everywhere to repent.*" If we do not repent when we sin, our prayers are not going to be heard.

God's standard is holiness, nothing less. Therefore, His first condition is a pure heart. In Isaiah 1:15 God says: *"I will hide mine eyes ... I will not hear."* Unrepentant sin in our heart will make God close His ears to us; meaning He will hear our cry, but our unrepentant sin will restrain Him from responding. So, it is useless for us to pray when we are carrying a sin on our conscience which we have not yet acknowledged or confessed. Isaiah 59:1–2 says, *"Behold, the Lord's hand is not shortened, that it cannot save; nor His ear heavy, that it cannot hear. But your iniquities have separated you from your God; and your sins have hidden His face from you, so that He will not hear."*

God wants to commune with us, so, out of His love for us, we have an advocate with the Father, Jesus Christ the righteous (1 John 2:1). Jesus now lives to make intercession for us (Hebrews 7:25) and we can confess our sins to Him, and He will readily forgive us (1 John 1:9). So, no one need to hold on to sin.

There is no point praying while we have ill feelings toward others because God will not hear us. So, despite the harm done to you, despite the depth of the pain, you must summons the Holy Spirit to help you confess, repent, and walk away from any inclination toward ill feelings for your offender.

Your Response

Read Psalm 51:10 and meditate on it. **Think** about what God means by a clean heart and think about what could be in your heart to make it unclean. **Pray** King David's prayer (Psalm 51) for a clean heart. **Ask** Jesus to reshape your thinking and your feelings toward others, especially your offender, so that His ears will be open to your prayers.

Day 11:
Who Is Without Sin?

⁴ and said to Jesus, "Teacher, this woman was caught in the act of adultery. ⁵ In the Law Moses commanded us to stone such women. Now what do you say?" ⁶ They were using this question as a trap, in order to have a basis for accusing him. But Jesus bent down and started to write on the ground with his finger. ⁷ When they kept on questioning him, he straightened up and said to them, "Let any one of you who is without sin be the first to throw a stone at her."

—John 8:4-7 (NIV)

It is interesting that when the topic of forgiveness comes up, people often talk from the offended's perspective — the wrong that was done to them. Often very little if any attention is given to the fact that we are sometimes the offender. No one is without sin, we are all flawed; therefore, at some point in life, we all will offend someone.

When the woman was caught in adultery, it goes without question that she was guilty and worthy of punishment. Similarly, when a person wrongs us, they are guilty and are worthy of punishment. But note what Jesus did. Instead of exercising judgment, He exercised mercy. And He exercised mercy on the grounds that the people who so desperately wanted to stone the woman to death are themselves sinful just like the woman.

Could this be telling you that you must exercise mercy toward your offender? Could this be a reminder that you too are sinful and has been forgiven by your loving Father; therefore, you ought to forgive your offender and not be so determined to see them punished for what they did?

The law of Moses commanded that a woman caught in such an act be stoned to death. So, rightfully, she should be punished. The Word of God (i.e., Hebrews 13:4, Matthew 5:28; Exodus 20:14) says adultery is a sin. Therefore, if your spouse commits this sin, they have wronged God first, then you, and they deserve punishment.

This could be a deep wound for the husband or wife; as such, the offended may feel they have the right for justice. But note what Jesus did. He brought it to the attention of those who were determined to execute the law that they are not without sin. No one knows what Jesus wrote in the dust with His finger. But while He was writing, the people who were urged to stone the woman to death kept asking Jesus what He had to say about the matter. It was then that Jesus *"straightened up and said to them, "Let any one of you who is without sin be the first to throw a stone at her."* John 8:7b (NIV).

The offense this woman committed was not a personal assault against the crowd, so one could say this does not apply if someone wrongs me personally. They could argue that being wronged personally is entirely different from breaking the law of Moses or breaking a command of God.

The counsel here is that you must consider your ways before judging another or before seeking justice or retribution. It goes without saying that if we stop and think about how much we ourselves have sinned against God and our fellow brothers and sisters, we would be merciful to those who offend us.

Your Response

Pray for a soft heart toward your offender. **Pray** that God will fill your heart with love for your enemies. **Pray** that out of the love of God in you, you will show mercy to others. **Pray** that in your gratitude to God for His mercy toward you, you will in turn show mercy toward those who wrong you. **Read** Romans 12:19. **Ask** the Lord to help you, no matter the offense, to leave things in His hands. **Tell yourself** that the Lord will exercise vengeance for you in His own time and in His own way and you will not interfere.

Day 12: We Are All Members of One Body

²⁵ Therefore each of you must put off falsehood and speak truthfully to your neighbor, for we are all members of one body. ²⁶ "In your anger do not sin": Do not let the sun go down while you are still angry, ²⁷ and do not give the devil a foothold.

—Ephesians 4:25-27 (NIV)

This Scripture — Ephesians 4:25-27 — advises us to do several things *"for we are all members of one body."* (verse 25b). It is essential that we take heed to these things — put off falsehood and speak truthfully to our neighbor, do not sin even in our anger, do not let the sun go down while we are angry, and do not give the devil a foothold. We must be careful to do these things because if we violate them, we not only hurt ourselves, but we hurt the body of which we are a part.

The Apostle Paul was writing to the church of Ephesus when he wrote this letter, so "body" is referring to the body of Christ. When we lie to our brothers and sisters in Christ and become angry with and stay angry at them, we are hurting ourselves because we, along with our brothers and sisters are of the same body.

The Apostle Paul's discussion of the members of the Body in 1 Corinthians 12: 15-21 (NIV) speaks very well to this issue. Here he explained that there is diversity in the Body, but we are one: "*¹⁵ Now if the foot should say, "Because I* *am not a hand, I do not belong to the body," it would not for that reason stop being part of the body. ^{16} And if the ear should say, "Because I am not an eye, I do not belong to the body," it would not for that reason stop being part of the body. ^{17} If the whole body were an eye, where would the sense of hearing be? If the whole body were an ear, where would the sense of smell be? ^{18} But in fact God has placed the parts in the body, every one of them, just as he wanted them to be. ^{19} If they were all one part, where would the body be? 20 As it is, there are many parts, but one body. The eye cannot say to the hand, "I don't need you!" And the head cannot say to the feet, "I don't need you!"*

In other words, all the members of the Body are inter-connected and mutually dependent on each other. The Body cannot operate at its full capacity without the cooperation and support of the other members of the Body. That being the case, if one member of the Body is negatively affected, then the entire Body is affected. If our right arm is affected, it may not affect our digestive system or our sight. But rest assured, with a dysfunctional arm, the body will not operate at its best. The same thing applies to the spiritual body. If one member of the Body is offended, it affects the entire Body by causing some level of dysfunction.

Your job is to do your part to ensure the health and well-being of the Body. A good place to start is with Ephesians 4:25-27. Should you have reason to be angry at a brother or sister, you are instructed here to address it promptly so that the devil does not have legal right to establish himself in the situation that caused the anger. And should you be tempted to lie to or on a brother or sister in the Lord, do not do it. These behaviors will only give the devil a foothold in the Body.

Your Response

Look at the Church, especially your local assembly and the churches with which you interact as your family. Indeed, these dear brothers and sisters in Christ are your family. Now, **examine** your relationship with them. Are you doing all you can to ensure a healthy relationship with them? **Ask**, God to show you anything you are doing that makes room for the devil to wreak havoc in the family. **Pray** specifically into Ephesians 4:25-27. You want to be void of deception, you want to control your anger, and you want to deal with issues without delay so that there are no lingering frictions between you and anyone in the Body.

Day 13: Unforgiveness Hides the Face of God

But your iniquities have separated you from your God; your sins have hidden his face from you, so that he will not hear.

—Isaiah 59:2 (NIV)

There are several accounts in Scripture where God commands us to forgive. A few examples are Ephesians 4:32, Matthew 6:14 and 15, Colossians 3:13, Mark 11:25, and Luke 17:3. Although we have free will to choose, if we want to live like children of God, forgiveness is not optional, it is a mandate. This makes forgiveness a law of God and as stated in 1 John 3:4, when we transgress the law of God, we sin. Therefore, unforgiveness is a sin.

Here we see in Isaiah 59:2 that our sins — including unforgiveness — will hide the face of God from us. Unforgiveness will separate us from God. Do you want to be apart from God? Do you want God to hide his face from you, so that He does not hear your prayers?

We know that God is not human, He is a Spirit (John 4:24); therefore, He does not have a face. But Isaiah is applying human characteristics to God — even though He does not have them — so we can better understand and relate to Him. We also know that God is omnipresent. So, this is not referring to God being everywhere. The withdrawing of God's presence here by Him hiding His face is referring to His covenant presence. We see this in the Garden of Eden where God fellowshipped with Adam and Eve. We also see His covenant presence with the children of Israel in the wilderness — a pillar of cloud by day and fire by night.

The face of God represents his covenant presence and favor. His face is turned toward His people to bless and sustain them (Psalm 67:1; Daniel 9:17). Every Believer's desire is for the face of God to "shine" upon him or her. But there are times when God hides His face, or turns His face away from us. This is typically an act of discipline or judgment, where God withholds interaction or experiences with us so we may sense our need for His grace and power and seek Him anew. This is why the psalmists sometimes cried out, *"How long will you hide your face from me?"* (Psalm 13:1).

The face of God shines upon us in blessing, and turns away from us in discipline. Sin separates us from Him, so when we are unforgiving, He disciplines us. He may feel distant from us, and His grace may be delayed. But thanks be to our loving Heavenly Father, He is not far off, neither is His love for us contingent upon how we act. God's love is everlasting and there is nothing we can do to make Him love us less than He already loves us. God's love is complete, and nothing can separate us from it. But when we sin, we forfeit His closeness, the intimacy He so deeply desires to have with us.

Your Response

Unforgiveness is unlikely if you have deep intimacy with God. **Pray** for deeper intimacy with God. Intimacy comes by spending personal time with God, spending time with people who are in love with God, and by getting to know God more in His Word. **Pray** for the discipline to have a steady prayer life and Word study life. A deep loving relationship with God will make you obey His laws (including forgiveness). A deep loving relationship with Him will make you want His covenant presence with you always. **Pray** for grace to live a life that entertains His covenant presence.

Day 14:
No Root of Bitterness

^{14} Make every effort to live in peace with everyone and to be holy; without holiness no one will see the Lord. ^{15} See to it that no one falls short of the grace of God and that

no bitter root grows up to cause

trouble and defile many.

—Hebrews 12:14-15 (NIV)

If there is no root, there will be no plant. Roots absorb and feed trees and plants with water and nutrients, and they secure the tree in the ground. Therefore, a tree or plant cannot exist without roots.

Hebrews 12:15 gives practical steps Christians must take in response to hardship. Prior verses encourage Believers to "hold fast" (Hebrews 3:6; 10:23) in the face of struggles. Most of the suffering we endure as Christians are not as severe as they could be (Hebrews 12:4), but whether severe or not, we must endure difficult and painful situations.

We must understand that God's intentions toward us are always good (Jeremiah 29:11), so, these situations that we wish never happened are for our good. They can groom us into becoming more mature in faith (Hebrews 12:11). And while we grow in faith and spirituality, we must be keenly aware of how we interact with other Believers, especially those who are weaker in faith than us.

Hebrews 12:14 mentions the need to live in peace, as well as the importance of pursuing holiness. This may be pointing to the elements of our faith walk that ensure there is no root of bitterness in us — peaceful relationships with our neighbors and a life of holiness unto God. Many other New Testament Scriptures, such as 1 Corinthians 5:11, 1Peter 1:15, Galatians 2:20, and Romans 12;1-2 highlight the importance of not tolerating sin in our lives.

The "root of bitterness" mentioned in this New Testament Scripture points to a metaphor used in Deuteronomy 29:18–19, an Old Testament Scripture. There, the people of Israel were warned against assuming they would be blessed and protected by God, regardless of their willful rebellion. The Scripture warns against *"a root that beareth gall and wormwood."* The New King James Version refers to gall as bitterness. Yahweh was warning His people against giving way to any root of bitterness growing in them, and this only came about from disobeying God. Old Testament Hebrew uses the word "bitter" as a reference to poison. Here, the "bitter roots" are said to cause trouble and it defiles others. People who are bitter contaminate or influence others in like same manner. They cause arguments and lead others into sin.

Bitterness is deeply buried in the soul. It is a root; therefore, it is not readily seen with the naked eyes. But even though it is not readily seen, it is still there, and it is deadly. It is a hidden, vicious cancer that needs very little cultivation, and it is very difficult to remove. It grows quickly, only to destroy from the inside out. To get rid of bitterness, you must kill the root.

The Old English source of the word bitterness is bitan, meaning "to bite." This could suggest two things. One, bitterness makes a person unfriendly and bite at (be mean to) others. Two, people become bitter because of the bite (hurt) from the infraction done to them.

If we go with the second option, bitterness would be like being bitten by the old serpent Satan, releasing his venom and poison into our heart and life. Acts 8:23 (NIV) supports the fact that bitterness is a venom, that it is poisonous: *"For I see that you are full of bitterness and captive to sin."*

Remember bitterness is a root. It grows like weed. It spreads and can potentially take over the container in which it is growing. In other words, bitterness can consume the carrier. Bitterness can grow like a vine and literally choke the life out of anything else trying to grow in that area. Bitterness will tie you to that person or event that hurt you. Unless you kill the root, you will carry the weight of the offense throughout your life. You do not want that to be you.

Your Response

Pray for a submitted will to God so that you can avoid harboring unforgiveness. Unforgiveness leads to bitterness. The root of bitterness is watered with an unhealthy thought life. **Do not** mentally rehearse what was done to you, but instead, **think** upon things that are pure, lovely, of good report, virtuous, and true. **Read** Philippians 4:8 in various Bible versions, **pray** about it, and **meditate** on it.

Day 15:
Hatred Stirs Up Conflict

Hatred stirs up conflict, but love

covers over all wrongs.

—Proverbs 10:12 (NIV)

Love and hate are opposite, and their effects are opposite as well. Christians are called to love everyone, even those who hurt and betray us. Hatred is a very strong term, and it is not of God; it is of the Devil. A few synonyms for hate are detest, loathe, despise, abhor, and execrate. But hate also means distaste, dislike, resentment, aversion, hostility, ill will, and ill feeling. Compared to the first list of synonyms, perhaps, we can better digest these terms.

If you harbor unforgiveness, meaning after being hurt, you expect retribution, no matter how long it takes, it is very likely you will end up disliking and resenting your offender. You will likely have ill will and ill feelings toward your offender, and could even become hostile to them. What you must know is, revenge-seeking never have a good ending. It only proliferates anger and escalates a cycle of retaliation. Choosing to respond in love, instead, is far more effective and should be the response of every follower of Christ.

When you cannot forgive your offender, you could come to despise them. You will despise them because your desire for justice is not met. In your eyes, your offender is not held accountable for what they did to you. This ill feeling toward your offender could be expressed openly or in subtle passive ways. You could find yourself unintentionally arguing and tearing down the person or instead of speaking well of the person, you could find yourself speaking negatively about them. These behaviors will stir up conflict. These behaviors which are evidence of hatred, will divide and disrupt fellowship.

Hatred will destroy your testimony and cause you to discredit Christianity. Hatred serves the Devil not God. Love, on the other hand, covers faults and sins. It is important to note that love does not overlook sin. Love does not ignore sin or cover it up. Love tries to find common ground and ways to work together, even with the offender. Love does not expose the offender's ways; it waits patiently for the offender to see the error of his way and repent. Love is willing to forgive. In fact, love forgives. As far as it is possible and reasonable, love pursues unity and peace (John 17:21; Romans 12:18).

Love — not hate — is what identifies us as disciples of (belonging to) Jesus. He said, "*A new commandment I give to you, that you love one another: just as I have loved you, you also are to love one another. By this all people will know that you are my disciples, if you have love for one another*" (John 13:34–35, emphasis added).

Cain did not do what is right because he had ill will and ill feelings toward his brother. He hated his brother. When "*Cain was very angry and his face was downcast*" (Genesis 4:5, NIV), because God looked more favorably on Abel's sacrifice, God said, "*Why are you angry? Why is your face downcast? If you do what is right, will you not be accepted? But if you do not do what is right, sin is crouching at your door; it desires to have you, but you must rule over it.*" (Genesis 4:6-7, NIV).

To "do what is right" we must love. When we love we cannot hate, and when we love we keep God's law. Jesus said the entirety of the law is summed up in the command to "*Love the Lord your God with all your heart and with all your soul and with all your mind*" (Matthew 22:37, NIV), and "*to love your neighbor as yourself*" (Matthew 22:39, NIV). Your neighbor incudes those who love you and are kind to you as well as those who mean you no good and have done you harm.

If you find even a shadow of hatred in your heart you ought to go to the throne of grace and ask God to fill your heart with His love. You cannot bear hatred and get away with it. Hate will always lead to evil deeds. But love, which is more powerful than hate, will always lead to good deeds and "cover all wrongs."

Your Response

THE SPOKEN WORD ON FORGIVENESS. A 40-DAY DEVOTIONAL

Read Matthew 22: 37-39 and think about what it means to love your neighbor as yourself. **Think** about who constitute your neighbor. **Think** specifically about anyone with whom you may have a strained relationship. **Examine** your affection for that person. How do you really feel about them? Are your thoughts about them good? **Ask** God to fill your heart with love for them.

YOUR DUTY TO FORGIVE

Day 16: How Much Do You Love Him?

If ye love me, keep my commandments.

—John 14:15 (KJV)

God is love. 1 John 4:16b (NIV) says, *"God is love. Whoever lives in love lives in God, and God in them"* and 1 John 4:8 says, *"Whoever does not love does not know God, because God is love."* A widely known verse and probably the best description of God's love for mankind is John 3:16 (KJV, emphasis added): *"For God so loved the world, that he gave his only begotten Son, that whosoever believeth in him should not perish, but have everlasting life."* Another verse that speaks directly of God's love for us is Romans 5:8 (NIV): *"But God demonstrates his own love for us in this: While we were still sinners, Christ died for us."*

Both John 3:16 and Romans 5:8 show us that God did something to express His love for us. God not only talk about how much He loves us, but He has also actively shown and still shows the depth of His love for us. God wants us to love Him back. He wants a relationship with us. He wants each one of us to cultivate our own personal relationship with Him.

To God, love is an action word. As He has done (John 3:16; Romans 5:8), we must do something to show our love for Him. John 14:15 tells us what we must do to show God that we love Him. The verse clearly states that we must obey Him if we love Him. Obey what? John 14:23 says, *"Anyone who loves me will obey my teaching."* Here again we see Jesus linking obedience to His Word or His teaching to loving Him. Another terminology for Word or teaching is commandments.

It is a command, a teaching of Christ that we forgive those who wrong us. A few Scriptures where this command can be found are Matthew 6:14-15, Colossians 3:13, Luke 6:37, Matthew 18:21-22, and Mark 11:25. Forgiveness is a command of Christ and if we love Him, we will obey His commandments. Therefore, if we love the Lord, we will forgive those who offend us.

This is not an option. We cannot overlook this command because it is demanding and difficult to do. In some cases, it may even seem unfair. But this is a command just like any other command from Jesus. He said a meaningful way to show that we love Him is to obey His commands. So, how much do you love Him?

Jesus teaches that obedience to His commands is the primary sign of our love for Him. If we love the Lord we will keep His commandments out of our love for Him, not out of duty. When we love someone in the natural, we do all we can to please them and make them happy. Sometimes we make drastic changes simply because the person we love does not favor those things.

It is no different with the Lord. We do what He tells us to do because we love Him and want to please Him, not because we want Him to love us. He already loves us, and our behavior will not change that. As He has shown us with His deeds how much He loves us, we ought to show our love for Him with our deeds. So, will you forgive those who betray you and cause you undue pain, simply because you love the Lord? The guidance of the Holy Spirit is key for this love and obedience (John 14:16).

Your Response

John 14:16 says, "And I will pray the Father, and he shall give you another Comforter, that he may abide with you for ever." That Comforter is the Holy Spirit. **Pray** for the abiding presence of the Holy Spirit. **Pray** that the things in your life that may preclude the abiding presence of the Holy Spirit will be removed. You cannot walk this walk without the help of the Holy Spirit. **Pray** for an insatiable desire for God and a fervent love for Him that translates to obedience to His Word.

Day 17:
Restore Your Offender

Brethren, if a man be overtaken in a fault, ye which are spiritual, restore such an one in the spirit of meekness; considering thyself,

lest thou also be tempted.

—Galatians 6:1 (KJV)

In this verse (Galatians 6:1), the Apostle Paul is saying that the person who is stronger spiritually should help the weaker brother or sister who falls into sin. We sin when we do anything that contradicts the Word of God. So, a person could sin against God and at the same time offend a brother or sister in the Lord. In fact, whenever we do something that is an assault on anyone, we sin against God. So, the transgression or sin alluded to here in Galatians 6:1 could be an offense against someone that warrants forgiveness from the offended.

It is verses like these that make the command to forgive a high call. It is a tall order. This verse is telling us that if someone is overtaken with a fault, for example if they wrong you, you the offended, assuming you are more spiritually mature, should take on the responsibility of restoring that person. What! And we not only should restore them, but we should do so in the spirit of meekness. One reason we should do this is just in case we make the same mistake one day.

Any personal assault, being betrayed, lied on, cheated, or abused can be painful and can easily give a person reason to be unkind to their offender. But the Word of God demands otherwise from us. We in turn are instructed to minister to the person who hurt us. If we are spiritually mature enough, we should restore the person. We should reestablish the person to their position, probably back to their position in relation with us before the offensive act. Perhaps the offender is remorseful and is feeling like a failure due to their conduct, our job is to build them up and encourage them so that they can be reinstated.

The word translated "restore" here is katartizete, used in common Greek as a reference to resetting broken bones, and in the New Testament for mending fishing nets. To "restore" something is to make it whole and functional again. In the case of offense, you would be proactive in restoring the relationship with the offender that was compromised due to their hurtful behavior. You would seek to reset the relationship back to its original state. This reminds me of Romans 12:18 (NIV, emphasis added): "*If it is possible, as far as it depends on you, live at peace with everyone.*" It is everyone's responsibility, including the offended, to live in peace with everyone.

You should not only restore your offender, but you should do this in the spirit of meekness. While you help this brother or sister, your offender, you must do so gently, not harsh or condemning. You were wronged, so you may think you "have the right" to handle the matter differently, but we are advised to handle the matter with the understanding that you could be the one at fault. This is not something anyone can do in their own strength. You need the help of the Holy Spirit to minister to the person who set out to harm you and might have done so.

Your Response

Read Romans 12:18 and Psalm 34:14. **Think** of your general response when anyone wrongs you, do you try to make peace with them? If so, in what way do you seek and pursue peace? If not, what changes do you need to make to come in alignment with the Scriptures. **Ask** God to show you the weak areas in your life that would render you spiritually immature or not as mature as you ought to be.

Day 18
A Gentle Versus
A Harsh Word

A gentle answer turns away wrath, but a harsh word stirs up anger.

—Proverbs 15:1 (NIV)

A viable precursor to someone hurting another person is an argument. But here the wise Solomon is telling us how we can avoid arguments, or how we should respond to anger. He says a soft or gentle answer can defuse a potentially explosive situation. In this context, the word "wrath" means rage. This is the kind of volatile anger that could escalate to physical conflict. When we are angry or even feel insulted, we may respond in the same manner that caused us to become angry. However, if we choose to respond to anger with harsh, hurtful words, we will make matters worse. Sharp, bitter responses only cause the enraged person's anger to escalate, resulting in further hostility.

In contrast, a calm, soft temper refuses to fight fire with fire. According to Solomon, the wise person answers the angry person gently, and that gentleness smothers the wrath. At minimum, a gentle, soft answer gives the fire of wrath no fuel to burn. A calm, polite response can take a great deal of tension out of an argument.

This type of behavior calls for spiritual maturity, self-control, wisdom, thoughtfulness, concern for the other person, and self-discipline. Romans 12:19–20 tell us not to avenge ourselves, but to know the Lord will repay the wrong. Our responsibility is to show kindness to our enemy: "*Do not be overcome by evil, but overcome evil with good*" (Romans 12:21, NIV).

Matthew 5:38-40 (NIV) says, "*³⁸ You have heard that it was said, 'Eye for eye, and tooth for tooth.' ³⁹ But I tell you, do not resist an evil person. If anyone slaps you on the right cheek, turn to them the other cheek also. ⁴⁰ And if anyone wants to sue you and take your shirt, hand over your coat as well*". There will be no fight if one person turns the other cheek. This teaching of our Savior Jesus is extremely rare. Rather than fight our enemies, we are to love them, bless them, do good to them, and pray for them (Matthew 5:39-43). Rather than hurl verbal or active insults back at them, we are to be kind to them.

Confrontational and insulting words that individuals often think of and verbalize when angrily confronted or when, because of pride, they feel they must defend themselves will cause fights to continue and escalate. Let this not be you. If you remember this teaching, you could stem arguments and potential offensive behaviors. It is true that "It takes two to fight." If either party were to stop fighting/arguing and show kindness, every fight would end, and some would not even become a fight. But a fight will get worse and do greater damage unless someone quickly bring the anger and contention to an end (Proverbs 17:14; 26:21). Let that person be you.

You can have a significant impact in propagating peace by ending fights and preventing offensive behaviors in your sphere of influence. Start in your marriage, your family, your place of employment, the marketplace, your church, or your neighborhood. You should be known by God and men in all your relationships and interactions as a peacemaker, not as harsh and argumentative.

Your Response

Sometimes the Lord asks things of us that requires deep personal change. Proverbs 15:1 may be that for you. But He is a merciful God, He gives us the grace to do whatever He requires of us. He never asks us to do anything that He does not empower us to do. So, perhaps you are the type of person that must have the last word. Perhaps, you fight fire with fire. Today, you are advised to **submit** to this Word, to **submit** to God. **Ask** the Lord to teach you how to be silent. **Ask** Him to teach you how to control your tongue and your emotions.

Day 19:
Even Sinners Love
Those Who Love Them

³² "If you love those who love you, what credit is that to you? Even sinners love those who love them. ³³ And if you do good to those who are good to you, what credit is that to you? Even sinners do that. ³⁴ And if you lend to those from whom you expect repayment, what credit is that to you? Even sinners lend to sinners, expecting to be repaid in full.

—*Luke 6:32-34 (NIV)*

Love is the missing element when a person intentionally wrongs another person. According to Romans 13:10 (NIV), *"Love does no harm to a neighbor."* And 1 Corinthians 13: 5 says, love does not dishonor others and does not think evil. So, love is not the premise for one's actions when they harm another person. However, even though the person who harms you does not love you, your Father in heaven requires that you love them. This is yet another reason the mandate to forgive is a high call. This is one reason it's a tall order.

We all have people in our lives who are kind to us. Some, because of their deep affection for us, will do almost anything for us. It goes without saying that it is quite easy to love these individuals. But Jesus raised the standard. He teaches that there is no credit in loving those who love us, even sinners do that. If these are the folks to whom we are selectively kind, we miss the mark because there is no benefit in doing good to someone who does good to us.

Jesus said to lend to our enemies, expecting absolutely nothing in return. Why? Because if you do this, you will be "sons of the Most High." Desiring and expecting are different. Desiring is wanting something. Nothing is wrong with that. We desire things every day. But expecting something could be bad because if, for example, you lend money to someone, and you expect to get it back, but the person does not repay you, you could do any number of things to get your money back. You could become angry, you could have ill feelings toward the person, or you could ask repeatedly for the money, which could then cause another problem. None of these responses are good but it is because you expected the money back. Jesus says, just give it to them.

As His children, we cannot live like or pattern the ways of sinners to any degree. Jesus places a high demand on us and we must aim at meeting the standards that He has set. This teaching is as far from the teachings of the world as the east is from the west, but as a child of the Most High, you must come in line with it.

Who can love in deed, not just in word, anyone who is intentionally unkind to them? In loving those who are hurtful to you in action, you do good to them, and you lend to them while not expecting anything back. In other words, you give to them. You do this because, first and foremost you love God, and in loving God, you obey Him. It is the love you have for God that will propel and empower you to love your enemy.

Who can do this? No one can do this without the abiding presence of the Holy Spirit in them. No one can do this without the love of God in them. No one can do this because they intellectually decide to do so. This is in direct contradiction to how the carnal man thinks and functions. Therefore, we must be rightly connected to the Vine and submitted to Him to come in alignment with this Word. But there's good news. You can do this, and so can I because the Greater One lives in us, and His grace is enough.

Your Response

Read Luke 6:32-36 in different versions and **meditate** on it. **Think** of situations where you had the opportunity to obey this command but failed. **Ask** the Lord to strengthen you so that at the next opportunity, you will obey Him. **Remind** yourself by reading 2 Corinthians 12:9 that God said, "My grace is sufficient for you, for my power is made perfect in weakness." Tell the Lord, you want to obey Him but in fact, you are weak. Tell Him you do not have the strength to do it. That will give Him room to strengthen you because in your weakness, He is made strong on your behalf. Talk to Him. Be transparent with Him. He is ready to help and strengthen you.

Day 20: Confess To and Pray for One Another

Therefore confess your sins to each other and pray for each other so that you may be healed. The prayer of a righteous person is

powerful and effective.

—James 5:16 (NIV)

To confess is to admit, reveal, or acknowledge one's guilt of a wrongdoing or sin. The word "fault" in the King James Version of the Bible is "sin" in the New International Version, and it is "trespass" in the New King James Version. The Greek translation for "trespass" is "paratoma." This word refers to a trespass that a person commits that offends or affects another person in a negative way.

A general interpretation of this Scripture is, we should confide our problems to a close, trusted friend so that he or she can help us by praying to God for help in overcoming them. By instructing us to confess our faults to one another, James does not mean that we should reveal every sin and weakness to everyone in the congregation. But if we consider the meaning of the word "paratoma," James is speaking specifically of acts that offend or affect others in a negative way.

In writing to an audience comprised of Jewish and Gentile Believers, James states that it should be common practice for Christians to confess our sins to each other and to pray for each other. Therefore, when we commit an act that offends or affects anyone in a negative way, we should be honest about our wrongdoing. The Scripture says, "<u>so that</u> *you may be healed*" (emphasis added). It is clear here that our healing depends on this act.

In addition to confessing to one another, we should pray for one another. It need not be known by others that we are praying or even asked of us to pray. We may notice a brother or sister struggling with a problem, and rather than discussing their flaw with others, we should get on our knees to petition God on their behalf. James assures us that when we pray fervently, it will make a difference. Prayer works! We will be healed when we pray fervently and with the right heart condition.

Some Bible scholars interpret the word "healed" here as a reference to healing from physical illness. Others understand it to mean healing from emotional conditions such as discouragement and from spiritual weakness. In either case, this healing requires two things from Christians: confession our sins to each other and fervent prayer for each other.

In this context, I am considering "healed" to mean holistic healing, especially spiritual, emotional, relational, and mental healing. In keeping with our discussion of God's spoken word on forgiveness, if we confess our faults and pray for one another in times of interpersonal conflicts, we will be healed emotionally. If we pray sincerely and fervently for the person who hurt us, we will be healed, and so will our offender.

If we are transparent and honest with one another when we hurt each other, our relationships will be much more wholesome and healthier. If we confess our faults to one another, disputes will not worsen and hurt will not fester. If we confess our faults to one another, we will be healed of bitterness, and we will be better off spiritually.

Your Response

One of the biggest hindrances to obeying this Word could be pride. You could be overthinking what the other person will think of you if you confess your faults. You may think you will look weak or perhaps the person to whom you confess may think they have the upper hand. But **think** of the benefits and the abundant blessings that come with obeying God's Word. **Pray** against pride. **Make** the resolution to obey God, not man. **Decide** that you will care most about what God says and thinks about you, not what man thinks or say about you. Your goal is to please God, not man. **Do** everything you can to ensure that.

Day 21: Privately Point Out Their Fault

If your brother or sister sins, go and point out their fault, just between the two of you. If they listen to you, you have won them over.

—Matthew 18:15 (NIV)

There are many ways in which a person can handle disputes, some healthy and others unhealthy; some constructive and some entirely destructive. When we act in our interest without consideration of the next person, or when we act in flesh (in our own interest irrespective of what the Word of God says), we will undoubtedly handle conflicting situations in a destructive manner.

It would be destructive and against the teachings of Jesus if we talk to everyone about what a brother or sister did to us but not to the offender. It would also be against Scripture if the first time we talk to the offender about the matter is in a public forum in the hearing of other individuals. The goal is to *"keep the unity of the Spirit in the bond of peace"* (Ephesians 4:3), not to shame or humiliate anyone, so it is important to follow the teachings of Jesus.

Jesus teaches that if another Believer sins against us, the first step is always to have a private conversation with the person. This could be the most effective approach to obtaining peace between the parties if done in the spirit of meekness and love.

When done in this manner, the chances of the situation getting worse is significantly reduced. If the person who was wronged approaches the offender with an expressed desire for peace and reconciliation, the offender will more likely acknowledge and repent of their offense against the other person, especially if the offender has a heart for God.

Yes, the person has consciously or unconsciously offended you. They hurt your feelings and have sinned against you. However, if you react to your offender with negative remarks or an unkind attitude or behavior, it is very unlikely that the outcome will be good. Quite possibly, the situation will worsen.

Jesus' teaching requires and is rooted in humility and grace. The Lord Jesus demonstrated true humility for us. He set aside His eternal glory to seek and to save that which was lost, you and me. Jesus died to reconcile us back to the Father.

Like Jesus, our goal must be reconciliation. Therefore, we should address the issue in private and in love, humility, and grace to prevent it from festering into bitterness or resentment.

No matter how or to the degree we have been wronged, it is important to follow the scriptural guidelines. Above all, we address the issue in private, and while doing so, our words should be seasoned with salt, and our attitude should reflect Christ-like humility, gentleness, and patience. As well, we should be ready to receive correction in truth and in love.

However deeply we have been wronged we should never permit ungodly communication to proceed out of our mouth. The word of God says, *"A word fitly spoken is like apples of gold in pictures of silver"* (Proverbs 25:11, KJV).

Words that are spoken in grace are more likely to divert an angry response because *"A wholesome tongue is a tree of life: but perverseness therein is a breach in the spirit."* (Proverbs 15:4, KJV), but harsh words and words that are spoken in haste stir up anger and strife.

Your life ought to reflect Christ's gentle humility. You must learn to speak the truth in love to your brothers and sisters in Christ. I pray you will listen to the wise teachings of Jesus your Lord so that you may *"grow in grace, and in the knowledge of our Lord and Savior Jesus Christ. To him be glory both now and for ever"* (2 Peter 3:18, KJV).

Your Response

THE SPOKEN WORD ON FORGIVENESS. A 40-DAY DEVOTIONAL

Adherence to this teaching requires self-control. You may be quick to speak or act because of the wrong that is done to you, but hear the Word of the Lord today. **Seek** peace and **pursue** it, and in doing so, **treat** your offender with gentleness and love. **Ask** the Lord to give you the discipline to respond in a timely manner and in a Christlike manner when you are wronged. **Ask** the Lord to give you a desire for unity in the Spirit with your brothers and sisters in Christ.

Day 22:
Repay Evil With Blessing

Do not repay evil with evil or insult with insult. On the contrary, repay evil with blessing,

because to this you were called so that

you may inherit a blessing.

—*1 Peter 3:9 (NIV)*

As humans, we instinctively operate in the Adamic carnal nature. We intuitively think to respond with evil when evil is done to us and we naturally hurl back insults when insulted. Without the transformative work of the Holy Spirit in us, we will be revengeful, merciless, and unforgiving. But the inner work of the Holy Spirit can *"cleanse our consciences from acts that lead to death, so that we may serve the living God!"* (Hebrews 9:14b, KJV).

Can you think of a time when someone did you wrong and the first thing you thought of was to do something good to or for them in return for what they did to you? Can you think of a time when someone cursed you or insulted you and the first thing you thought of was to respond with kind or complimentary words, or words that bless them? I applaud you if that is your mode of operation, but most of us do not routinely respond in such a way.

If the Holy Spirit is not abiding in you, and not only abiding but governing you, you will render evil for evil and insults for insults. Abiding means the Holy Spirit lives in you. It means you prepare a place of habitation for Him, and He lives there. He does not make sporadic visits or stay for short periods of time; your heart is His home. Ruling or governing means He has the final say. He dictates how you act, when you act, how you speak, what you say, when you speak, and to whom you speak. He dictates your every move. We all need the abiding and ruling presence of the Holy Spirit in us so that we can willingly pay evil with good and respond to insults with blessings.

Injustice is never pleasant. It does not feel good to be lied on, cheated, molested, betrayed, abused, disrespected, or misjudged. The way of the world and our human nature is to strike back with the same hurtful treatment we receive. But for followers of Christ, revenge is never the right thing to do. Followers of Jesus Christ are not allowed to "get even." We simply cannot because that is not characteristic of Christ. Jesus *"was oppressed and afflicted, yet he did not open his mouth; he was led like a lamb to the slaughter, and as a sheep before its shearers is silent, so he did not open his mouth"* (Isaiah 53:7, NIV). All our ways must mirror His.

Instead of repaying evil with evil or insult with insult, Peter commands us to "bless," or speak well of our offenders. Therefore, the godly thing to do when someone wrongs you is to pray for them. Ask God to help them succeed in their endeavors and pray that they would experience God's favor.

Now, this will sound absurd to the natural man, in fact, the natural man would think this is a foolish thing to do. Why would anyone ever do such a thing for someone who has hurt or insulted them? Peter answered that question in 1 Peter 2:21–25. We respond with a blessing when given evil, because that is what Jesus did for us, and He is our example. We are to strive daily to be like Christ in all things.

Peter adds two ideas here. First, as followers of Christ, we are "called" to this work of giving blessings in exchange for evil and insults. That is part of our purpose as God's set-apart people on earth. This is a powerful ingredient for inner healing and reconciliation, since only forgiveness can break the cycle of revenge.

Second, as we give blessings for insults and evil, we will obtain or "inherit" a blessing for ourselves. This blessing may mean eternal life or, more likely, this blessing is additional rewards from God in this life and/or in the life to come. Do you want to inherit that blessing?

Your Response

Examine your life. **Look** to see if you tend to take matters in your own hands when people wrong you. Are you the kind to want to have the last word? Are you the kind to want to get even? **Be honest** with yourself. **Ask** the Holy Spirit to help you. **Surrender** your ways to Him. **Let** the Holy Spirit become the ruler, yes, the dictator of your life. **Submit** fully to Him. **Acknowledge** that you are not your own and **leave** everything to Him. He will fight your battles and you will inherit a blessing.

Day 23:
Leave Your Gift
On The Altar

²³ Therefore, if you are offering your gift at the altar and there remember that your brother or sister has something against you, ²⁴ leave

your gift there in front of the altar.

First go and be reconciled to them;

then come and offer your gift.

—Matthew 5:23-24 (NIV)

The Word of God cannot lie. Isaiah 55:8-9 say, *"For my thoughts are not your thoughts, neither are your ways my ways, saith the Lord. For as the heavens are higher than the earth, so are my ways higher than your ways, and my thoughts than your thoughts."* Matthew 5:23-24 exemplify how far the thoughts of God are from the thoughts of man. From man's perspective, the question would be why should I be the one responsible for reconciling with the brother or sister who has something against me? If my heart is clear towards my brother or sister, why can't I just worship my God and leave the responsibility for reconciliation to the brother or sister? After all, he/she is the one that has something against me.

Matthew 5:23-24 line up very well with Romans 12:18 (NIV) which states, *"If it is possible, as far as it depends on you, live at peace with everyone."* Here we see the responsibility for maintaining peace with our brothers and sisters being placed on us. It is not solely your offender's responsibility to make peace, it is also your responsibility to do so. Although you suffered the fate of the offender, God puts it on you to make peace with the offender. Only God thinks like that.

It could be that your brother or sister has something against you because of something you have done to them. That would make you the offender. But either way, the Word of God is telling us that we cannot worship Him while having unresolved issues with anyone.

Isaiah 55:8-9 remind us that when we come before God in worship, we must recognize that we are invited in His presence and are deemed His child only because of His forgiveness, mercy, and grace. So, we cannot presumptuously worship Him and receive this forgiveness, mercy, and grace when we are not in a right standing with others. For us to be right with God, we must be right with each other.

Four of the Ten Commandments focus on the Lord and the remaining six focus on our relationship with each other. The Scriptures have many accounts of and place much emphasis on the fact that God does not accept worship from those who mistreat or exploit others. Jesus teaches that we will not be forgiven if we ourselves do not forgive others. He even says that we will be judged by the same standard by which we judge others. So, regardless of how deep, how moving, how stirring, how spiritual our worship may seem, if we have unresolved issues with anyone and we do not try to settle the matter with them, God will not accept our worship.

Your Response

Ask the Lord to forgive you for harboring grudges, for saying unkind things, and for being insensitive to the hurts you have caused others. **Make** the decision to forgive anyone who have hurt you and **give up** any claim against your brothers and sisters in Christ or anyone who have hurt you. **Resolve** to live peaceably with them from hereon. Now, **think** of anyone that could possibly have something against you, and **go** to them to make it right prior to going before the Lord to worship Him.

Day 24:
Living Peacefully with Others Depends on You

18 If it is possible, as far as it depends on you, live at peace with everyone. 19 Do not take revenge, my dear friends, but leave room for God's wrath, for it is written: "It is mine to avenge; I will repay," says the Lord. 20 On the contrary: "If your enemy is hungry, feed him; if he is thirsty, give him something to drink. In doing this, you will heap burning coals on his head."

—Roman 12:18-20 (NIV)

Upon reading Scriptures like Romans 12:18, it appears as if the Father is asking too much of us. From a natural perspective, one would ask why it is dependent upon me to live peacefully with everyone, especially if the person has wronged me. But this just goes to show that our God is a God of unconditional, relentless love, and that He is a God of peace. Also, it shows that His Word, His teachings, and the requirements that He places on us depict who He is.

Romans 12:18 says if possible, as far as it depends on *us*, and in this case, I am referring to the "us" as the offended, that is persons who have been hurt by another individual. The offended must do what they can to live peacefully with their offender. So even after the offender has committed the wrong, the charge is placed upon the offended to exert all the effort possible to make peace with the offender. This does not mean the offender is not held accountable, or has no responsibility to make peace, but based on what verses 19 and 20 say, it is evident that the directive in verse 18 is for the offended.

The word "possible" shows up in this verse — If it is *possible*, as far as it depends on you — because the Father knows that in some cases, it will not be possible to make peace with the offender. We must embrace this truth but at the same time, we must try do everything we can to make peace. We should also know that peace does not look the same way in every situation. Much of this requires godly wisdom because some offenders are not amenable to peacemaking, but in our efforts to make peace, our intent must be to move farther from discord and closer to harmony.

Verse 19 suggests that though you have forgiven the offender, they will face the wrath of God. The offender will not go unjudged by God. Some people find delight in this verse, but this should give you no reason to rejoice. If you find cause for rejoicing here, it is a clear sign that you have not forgiven. The Word of God admonishes us that It is not our place to take revenge, we should leave room for His wrath. He will repay; not us, but at the same time we should not find joy in this fact.

Verse 20 further admonishes us to show kindness and love to our offender. The act of forgiveness is a gift of love. Specifically, verse 20 points to feeding our offender if they are hungry and giving them something to drink if they are thirsty. In your situation, you may not need to give food or drink to your offender, but you should be kind to them. You should go out of your way to be kind to them if there is a need. Though this should not be the reason for being kind to them, your kindness will awaken their conscience to the wrong they have done.

You must do these kind deeds with a pure motive. Anyone with a conscience cannot help but being convicted under these circumstances, but it should be the love of God in you that make you show kindness to your offender, not because you want to bring their attention to the wrong they did. If you have forgiven God's way, you will have no desire for the wrath of God to come upon them, for them to even be judged by God, or for their conscience to prick them. When you forgive God's way, you leave it all in the hands of the just and merciful God that you serve.

THE SPOKEN WORD ON FORGIVENESS. A 40-DAY DEVOTIONAL

What better way to show a person who has done you wrong that you are rooted in the love of Jesus Christ? What better way to show a person who has wronged you that you have written off the debt, that you have pressed the reset button, and that to you they are a beloved brother or sister in Christ, friend, family member, neighbor, or coworker?

Your Response

Ask God to make you a peacemaker. **Ask** Him to show you the approaches that are best to pursue peace with your offender. **Follow** the leading of the Lord. **Do not go ahead** of Him. **Say** only what He tells you to say and **do** only what He tells you to do. Also, when you say and do these thigs, it is equally important that you do them only when the Holy Spirit gives you the clearance to do them. If God directs your pursuit of peace and you follow His direction, all will be well.

DO AS GOD DID AND CONTINUES TO DO, FORGIVE

Day 25:
Forgive As The Lord Has Forgiven You

Bear with each other and forgive one another if any of you has a grievance against someone. Forgive as the Lord forgave you.

—*Colossians 3:13 (NIV)*

We are all born in sin and shaped in iniquity (Psalm 51:5); therefore, we are all flawed. No one is perfect. The Adamic nature to which we are all subject has rendered all of us faulty. Therefore, someone must tolerate us at some point in life. Someone must give us the gift of leniency when we behave in less-than-optimal ways. Likewise, we must tolerate someone else's imperfections.

We all fall short in the command given in Colossians 3:13 (NIV) to *"Bear with each other and forgive one another"* because far too often we lose patience with our brothers and sisters, even after one infraction. Our ability to endure one another is temporary and short-lived at best. Some people need more forbearance than others, but we all need someone to put up with us.

What we must consider is the degree to which Jesus tolerates us. He is longsuffering toward us, and it is not His desire than anyone perish, but that we all come to repentance (2 Peter 3:9). No one that ever lived or is living today can attest that they have gone to the Lord with an issue that they have taken to Him on previous occasions, and He turned then away because He had lost patience with them. No one can testify that the Lord has told them He is tired of forgiving them of any wrong they have done and have confessed to Him. This is not the God we serve. He is forgiving, patient, longsuffering, merciful, and tender toward us.

Colossians 3:13 is telling us to bear with each other; to have leniency toward one another. We should not be so quick to write off or cut ties with the persons who wrong us. Should there be a grievance against anyone, we must be patient with the person, and we must forgive the person. Furthermore, we must do this in the *same way* the Lord does it for us. We must forgive *as* the Lord forgives us.

This certainly does not read like a suggestion or a request. The Scripture plainly states we should forgive one another. It is a command that we forgive *just as* God has forgiven us.

Our God is a forgiving God like none other. The death of Christ, His Son, grants forgiveness to all humankind, but it does not stop there. Christ lives forever to intercede for us (Hebrews 7:25). This tells us that the Father's act of forgiveness is not limited to Jesus' death on the cross. Because Jesus now sits at the right hand of the Father making intercession for us, His forgiveness is ongoing. Being at the right hand of the Father is the place of direct access and highest honor possible. Jesus sits there and is pleading and interceding on our behalf. When we err, Jesus is our advocate. When we err, He pleads our case.

We can see from Scripture what the Lord has done for us, and we are living in the rich blessings that His gift of love and forgiveness offers. We now have the privilege and the honor of blessing others by tolerating their imperfections and b forgiving them *just as* Christ has forgiven us.

To forgive just as Christ has forgiven us is to forgive without conditions, meaning despite the nature of the offensive act, we must forgive. There is no sin under the heavens that we can commit that is too heinous for God to forgive. To forgive just as Christ has forgiven us is to forgive without keeping a record of offenses. When Jesus forgives us, He casts our sins in the depths of the sea (Micah 7:19). Hebrews 8:12 tells us that God will be merciful to our unrighteousness, and He will not remember our sins and our iniquities. Jesus did it and is still doing it for us, and He requires that we do the same to others.

Without a doubt, this is a high call, but remember, you serve a just and faithful God. He has not and will never ask you to do anything that He does not provide the grace for you to do. He has made provisions for this command, and it is found in His Word, in the help of the Holy Spirit, and in relationship with Jesus Christ. You can if Christ lives in you!

Your Response

You are not Jesus, and you will never be Jesus, so a command such as this seems impossible. But God would not require it of you if it were impossible for you to do. A command like this must make you feel weak and helpless, and that is all right. That is exactly where God wants you to be because He wants you to depend on Him. Feeling weak and helpless is the best place to be because when you are weak, He becomes strong. To obey this command, you must **submit** to Him, you must **commit** your ways to Him, and you must **depend** on Him.

Day 26: Forgive As You Were Forgiven

24 As he began the settlement, a man who owed him ten thousand bags of gold was brought to him. 25 Since he was not able to pay, the master ordered that he and his wife and his children and all that he had be sold to repay the debt. 26 "At this the servant fell on his knees before him. 'Be patient with me,' he begged, 'and I will pay back everything.' 27 The servant's master took pity on him, canceled the debt and let him go.

—Matthew 18:24-27 (KJV)

How many times have you violated the Word of God, and you were called into account by the Holy Spirit? How many times have you repentantly asked God for forgiveness, and He cancelled your debt? How many times has He given you a fresh start? How many times do you feel that you have gone contrary to His Word so much that it seems quite difficult, near impossible to find your way back to Him, yet, even at these times of despair and feelings of worthlessness before Him, He restores you? These are all rhetorical questions because no one can keep record of the countless times God has forgiven and reestablished them. God in His unending love, restored you every time you went to Him. He restored you even when you felt like you have done it all and you cannot be put back together.

In this parable, the lord was attempting to settle his accounts with his servants. One of his servants owed him a huge sum of money (10,000 bags of gold, [$10 million or 60 million denarii]). When asked for the money, the servant begged the lord to forgive him. He pleaded for time to pay the debt and the lord took pity on him and instead of giving him extra time to pay the debt, he cancelled the entire debt, which means the servant no longer owed the money.

This same servant that was just forgiven of this unpayable sum of money soon found one of his fellow servants who owed him pittance (100 silver coins, $17 or 100 denarii) compared to the debt he owed the lord. The forgiven servant was merciless to his fellow servant. While demanding his silver coins from the fellow servant, he grabbed him by the throat and began choking him. And because the fellow servant could not pay the debt, he had the man placed in prison until he was able to pay back the debt.

This shows us the extremes to which unforgiveness can take us. Unforgiveness hardens our hearts, makes us self-centered and merciless, and it makes us completely ungrateful to God for His mercies toward us. The servant's plea for time to pay the debt of 60 million denarii was entirely unrealistic because according to Matthew 20:2, the daily wage of a worker in Palestine was a shilling, about 17 cents. With a daily wage of 17 cents, it would have taken the servant approximately 161,160 years to pay off this $10-million debt, even if every cent he earned was used to pay down the debt.

In this parable, the king represents God our Father and the indebted servant pictures each of us in the state of unforgiveness. The offenses that our brothers and sisters cause us are like the 100-denarii debt owed to the unmerciful servant and our transgressions against God's Word are like the $10-million debt to the lord.

The lord, who represents God, forgave the servant (us) of his debt (our sins) — a debt he could not (we cannot) pay. Yet the servant could not pardon a debt that was miniscule to the one for which he was forgiven.

There is nothing you can do that God will not forgive. Likewise, there should be nothing that anyone can do to you that you cannot forgive. No transgression against another person can exceed your transgressions or my transgressions against God, yet God has forgiven and continues to forgive. Consider the fact that you have new mercies every morning and that God never turns you away. Now think about how you would feel and what would happen to you if God started treating you the way you treat others. You would go with much of your sins unforgiven, you would not have the peace you have today because there would be uncertainties as to whether God will forgive or not. But thanks be to God, His mercy is unending. His mercies are from everlasting to everlasting, and He manifests them to you in more ways than you think.

Your Response

The first thing you need to forgive like God has forgiven you is a grateful heart. **Look over** your life, **consider** your ways and how graciously God has forgiven you every time you go to Him. **Ask** God to give you a grateful heart. **Ask** Him to remind you of some of the moments when He has done for you what no one else could do. Because He has been generously merciful to you, **ask** God to make you generous to others. **Ask** Him to make you forgive others *because* He has forgiven you. Jesus forgives like He does because He is love. **Ask** Him to fill you with His love.

Day 27: Forgive So That You May Be Forgiven

And when you stand praying, if you hold anything against anyone, forgive them,

so that your Father in heaven may

forgive you your sins.

—*Mark 11:25 (NIV)*

In life, it is common for people to behave in ways that offend us, but forgiving those who offend us is a struggle for most people. For many, holding a grudge feels natural, but the Bible mandates that we forgive.

Mark 11:25 sends a clear and very strong message that unforgiveness is extremely costly. This alone should be enough to make us forgive our offenders. The risk is far too great. The words *"so that"* tell me that our forgiveness from the Father is contingent upon us forgiving our offenders. We must forgive! There is no point praying while we have ill feelings toward others because God will not hear us, and He will not forgive us of our sins. Psalm 66:18 (KJV) is clear on this: *"If I regard iniquity in my heart, the Lord will not hear me."*

The forgiveness mentioned in Mark 11:25 — *"so that your Father in heaven may forgive you your sins"* — is contingent upon you forgiving your offenders, and this forgiveness of sins is not for salvation. Salvation is free. It is not conditional. So, we do not need to do anything to be saved. Jesus already paid the price for our sins; therefore, as reflected in Romans 10:9, all that is left for us to do is confess that Jesus is Lord and believe that He was raised from the dead, and we will be saved.

Note that Jesus was not talking to unbelievers. He was talking to His disciples, so this directly pertains to Believers. We cannot be deceived by believing this cannot apply to a child of God. This is the teaching of Jesus; it is for all who will listen — Believers and unbelievers — but Jesus was talking to His disciples. Though we are Believers, the law of sin that rules us prior to accepting salvation is not dead, it is merely subdued and is now overruled by the law of God. Consequently, we will err and will need forgiveness from God, but the forgiving of our sins depends on us forgiving those who wrong us. If you hold anything in your heart against anyone, get it resolved before praying.

For many and probably you, it is difficult to humble yourself and admit that you indeed are holding a grudge against a brother or sister. There may be concern that it will ruin your self-image, but think about how far from God this drives you every time you allow pride to restrain you from making things right. Nothing is worth putting yourself in a position that renders your prayers futile.

A major hindrance to answered prayers among Believers today is unforgiveness. Do not let this be said of you. There are so many people in church who pray, but because they harbor unforgiveness in their hearts, they do not receive the answers they expect from God. Mark 11:25 is clearly saying that if you do not forgive men their trespasses, neither will your Father in heaven forgive you your trespasses.

It is human nature to want to get even when treated unjustly, but as a follower of Christ, you are a new creature, old things have passed away (2 Corinthians 5:17). Therefore, as a Believer you strive to take on the nature of Christ. You must surrender to Christ and allow the finished work of the cross of Calvary to crucify your flesh and empower you to forgive others of their sin against you.

Your flesh must die, and you must allow the Holy Spirit to work through you to enable you to forgive those who hurt you. You cannot do this in human strength. You must be empowered by the Holy Spirit to do so, and He is ever so able and available to assist you.

Your Response

THE SPOKEN WORD ON FORGIVENESS. A 40-DAY DEVOTIONAL

Ask the Holy Spirit to help you **release** the people who have hurt you. Take the step, **reach** out to them, and **make peace** with them. The Bible says that as much as it lies within you, you should live peaceably with all men (Romans 12:18), so you have a responsibility to make amends. Furthermore, you should not let the sun go down with that unforgiveness still lurking around in you. You might not be able to resolve all issues before the literal sundown, but you should be careful not let it linger in you. **Listen** to the voice of the Holy Spirit as He is speaking to you right now, **forgive** and **move on** with your life.

Day 28: Forgiveness Is Conditional

¹⁴ For if ye forgive men their trespasses, your heavenly Father will also forgive you: ¹⁵ But if ye forgive not men their trespasses, neither will your Father forgive your trespasses.

—Matthew 6:14-15 (KJV)

Unforgiveness is one of those sins that do not have delayed consequences. Here we see one of the right now consequences of unforgiveness — if we do not forgive others, our Heavenly Father will not forgive us. Therefore, our forgiveness of sins is conditional; it is contingent upon our actions toward others. These words may not sit well with the way we have understood the gospel. God's forgiveness of our sins is founded in His love and grace; it has nothing to do with our works. There is nothing we can do to earn our salvation. So, one may ask, how can Jesus add an "If..." to the message? How can He make God's forgiveness dependent on what we do? But it is important to note that Jesus is referring to forgiveness of our offenses against another, not forgiveness for salvation.

Without doubt, this teaching that forgiveness is conditional could be difficult to comprehend or accept. 1 John 1:9 (NIV) says, *"If we confess our sins, he is faithful and just and will forgive us our sins and purify us from all unrighteousness."* Nothing is said here about us meeting a condition to be forgiven of our sins, neither does the verse say unforgiveness is a sin. Is unforgiveness included in the "sin" mentioned in 1 John 1:9?

We must note that this teaching is taught in a very specific sense. Jesus is saying that if we forgive the sins of others against us, our Heavenly Father will also forgive us of our sins against others. This is not the forgiveness of sins for salvation. This is specifically about forgiveness. If you do not forgive, you will not be forgiven (Matthew 6:15).

In the Sermon on the Mount, Jesus taught many very challenging principles. This is one of them. It is also extremely easy to misunderstand, if not considered carefully. If taken in isolation, Jesus seems to be saying we earn God's forgiveness after we forgive the sins of others against us, and we lose forgiveness when we refuse to forgive others. We cannot earn forgiveness from God. Forgiveness is a gift from God to us and we are expected to give that gift of love to others. God is displeased when we refuse to forgive others for the little offenses against us despite being forgiven by God for much greater offenses against Him (Matthew 18:23–35). The Word of God is clear that unforgiving attitudes are undoubtedly sinful.

Difficult or not, Jesus is speaking with the authority of God, and He always means what He says. We should never dismiss Jesus' teachings because they are hard to do, hard to understand, or hard to reconcile with other teachings. How can we dare go before God and ask Him to forgive us if we refuse to forgive others?

Forgiveness is based on love. God loves us enough to forgive us, and we should in like manner love others. We are forgiven to be agents of forgiveness. Forgiveness is just another attribute of being children of God. God's intentions have not changed. He designed you to imitate Him, and that is still His purpose.

Your Response

It is admittedly true that Matthew 6:14-15 is difficult to accept. We all know God to be loving, merciful, and forgiving. And we know we cannot work for or earn the blessing of forgiveness from God. To settle any uneasiness about this Scripture, **read** it in various versions and **read** commentaries on it. Also, **pray** to God for understanding and **pray** for an obedient spirit to do whatever the Holy Spirit shows you. Your goal is to imitate Christ. Your goal is for the world to see Jesus in you. If you obey the command to forgive your debtors, you will have met the "if" condition in Matthew 6:14-15.

Day 29:
Forgive and Be Forgiven

¹Judge not, and ye shall not be judged: condemn not, and ye shall not be condemned:

forgive, and ye shall be forgiven.

—*Luke 6:37 (KJV)*

Luke 6:37 may be the most widely quoted Bible verse. Even people who have never read the Bible seem to know this verse. You might have had someone hurl this verse at you when you deemed something right or wrong. But is this verse telling us that we should never judge a matter or a thing? The Word of God tells us to "*Turn from evil and do good*" (Psalm 37:27a, NIV). For us to obey this command, we must make judgments about what is evil and what is not.

A follower of Christ ought to obey what Psalm 37:27a says, and if we are going to do what it says, there must be some things that we should not do. For us to determine what we should and should not do, we must make judgments. So, since we make judgments all the time and are expected to do so, what is Jesus' teaching in Luke 6:37?

Jesus is teaching that we are to abstain from judging the motives of another person. For example, if someone does something that hurt you, and you say in response that "they meant to cause trouble" or they "intended to hurt me," you could be making judgments on things you do not know for sure. We judge when we don't have all the facts. We judge when we draw conclusions based on assumptions. The best way to avoid judging anyone, including your offender, is to talk to them, not about them.

Jesus also teaches that we should not condemn. We should not conclude that anyone is beyond hope, despite the harm they did to you. Despite how hostile and seemingly intolerable the person is, it is not your job to render them hopeless.

If you obey the first two commands in this verse — do not judge and do not condemn — the third command, which is to forgive, will be significantly easier to do. If you let God adjudicate the motive of your offender, if you see your offender as redeemable, meaning you see good in the person despite what they did, and if you see the relationship between you and the person as reconcilable, it will be much easier for you to forgive them.

The third command corroborates several Scriptures (Matthew 6:14-15, Ephesians 4:32, Colossians 3:13, and more). Without doubt, forgiveness places a high demand on us. It is widely viewed as one of the most difficult things that God asks of us. But it is hard when we try to do it in our own strength. It is hard when we are not submitted to God. James 4:7 (KJV) says, *"Submit yourselves therefore to God. Resist the devil, and he will flee from you."* So, we cannot resist the temptation to hold grudge and animosity against our offender if we do not submit to God.

If we are honest about the depth of our own sinfulness; if we truly grasp how offensive our sins are to God; if we really understand the magnitude of the gift of God's grace that has been given to us, we will forgive others. Many of us find it hard to forgive because we forget where God brought us from, and we are unaware of the condition of our own heart. If we come face-to-face with these things, we will forgive because we have been forgiven, and we have been forgiven of much worse than anything anyone can do to us. By forgiving, we pay the blessing we have received forward, and we open the door for forgiveness when we ourselves hurt someone.

Your Response

The thing that may be most needed to come in alignment with this Scripture is to be able to see others as God sees them. God's thoughts towards us are good. He has an expected end for His children. He has the final say about you and about your offender. So, what He says about your offender overrides what you say about them. **Ask** God to fill your heart with love for your offender. **Ask** Him to let you see them the way He sees them. We never come to a point where we are irreparable in God's eyes, and no one should be seen that way by anyone. Yes, you might have been violated, you might have been hurt, you might have been damaged, you might have been betrayed by this person, but has God written the person off? Absolutely not! And if He has not written them off, should you write them off? No! **Ask** Him to let you see your offender the way He sees them.

Day 30: Reaffirm Your Love By Forgiving

⁵ If anyone has caused grief, he has not so much grieved me as he has grieved all of you to some extent—not to put it too severely. ⁶ The punishment inflicted on him by the majority is sufficient. ⁷ Now instead, you ought to forgive and comfort him, so that he will not be overwhelmed by excessive sorrow. ⁸ I urge you, therefore, to reaffirm your love for him.

—2 Corinthians 2:5–8 (NIV)

It is verses like these that make me consider the command of our Father to forgive, a high call. Here the Father is not only commanding that we forgive our offenders, but He is also compelling that we comfort them. Based on 2 Corinthians 2:7–8, it is our job to comfort the offender when we forgive them, we ought to make sure our offender is not overwhelmed by excessive sorrow, and we must ensure our offender — the very person who has hurt us — feel loved by us. We are to respond to our offenders as such because according to verse 6, the punishment that is imposed on them by the majority — if the offense is public — is enough. God is commanding us to show mercy to our offenders.

It is very important that we understand that this is a command. It is not a suggestion. It reads, "*If anyone has caused grief, he has not so much grieved me as he has grieved all of you to some extent — not to put it too severely. The punishment inflicted on him by the majority is sufficient. Now instead, you <u>ought to</u> forgive and comfort him, so that he will not be overwhelmed by excessive sorrow. I urge you, therefore, to reaffirm your love for him.*" (emphasis added). The Greek word for ought is deh-on. It means necessary, behoove, must (needs be), or need. This is an expectation placed upon us by God. It provides no wiggle room, no matter what.

My beloved brothers, sisters, and friend, this high call of the Father is not natural; it is supernatural. One must be operating in the Spirit to forgive God's way. Forgiveness God's way cannot be done in the flesh. It is not a work of the mind or our intellect, neither is it an act of our emotions. It must be a work of the Holy Spirit.

So how do you comfort your offender and reaffirm your love to them? For a person to accept forgiveness, they must admit to doing wrong. If the person denies being wrong, you can forgive them, but they will not receive your forgiveness. In this case, you would release them from the offense, but there would be no opportunity for reconciliation.

It is probable that the person who admits to doing wrong will feel guilty or sorrowful about what they have done. This is where, you as the person who is offering forgiveness would comfort the offender and assure them that you are not holding what they have done against them. This will likely ease the sorrow and bring comfort to the offender. So, it may be important, when feasible and when fitting, to let the offender know that you are not keeping an account of their wrongdoing. This is particularly important for offenses that are public. Public wrongdoing will more likely bring shame and guilt than a private wrongdoing between two people. In fact, the scenario that led the Apostle Paul to send this word of council to the church of Corinth was a misdeed that was publicly known.

How can the offended reaffirm their love for the offender? Forgiveness is an act of love. It is said that to give and receive forgiveness is the highest act of love. God forgave us of our sins because He loves us. *"For God so loved the world, that he gave his only begotten Son, that whosoever believeth in him should not perish, but have everlasting life."* (John 3:16, KJV). It was love that made Him forgive us. He loves us so much that He was willing to pay the highest price to redeem us back to Him. Like we have experienced God's gracious act of redemption toward us as an act of love, if we forgive God's way, our offender will also experience our response as an act of love.

Your Response

Ask God to fill you with His love. Once you begin to operate out of His love, it will be much easier to forgive. Also, you must **relinquish control**. Sometimes we feel like because the other person did the wrong, we are better off, or we have control. **Make sure** you have no emotional, nonverbal, or behavioral control over the person. **Make sure** you convey to your offender in the clearest way you can that they owe you nothing.

HELP FOR YOU TO FORGIVE

Day 31:
You Need Faith to Forgive

³ Take heed to yourselves: If thy brother trespass against thee, rebuke him; and if he repent, forgive him. ⁴ And if he trespass against thee seven times in a day, and seven times in a day turn again to thee, saying, I repent; thou shalt forgive him. ⁵ And the apostles said unto the Lord,

Increase our faith.

—Luke 17:3-5 (KJV)

After establishing the fact that things that can cause offense will inevitably occur in life, Jesus, in His teachings to His disciples added that they must be on their guard. He taught them that if anyone sins against them, they must admonish the brother or sister; and if the person repents, they ought to forgive him. Jesus further added that if the person wrongs them seven times in one day and returns to them seven times saying, "I am sorry," they should forgive him. Immediately after hearing this teaching, the disciples asked Jesus to increase their faith.

In Matthew 18:21 (NIV) Peter came to Jesus, and said, *"Lord, how many times shall I forgive my brother or sister who sins against me? Up to seven times?"* Peter was answering his own question, but Jesus made the answer even clearer to Peter by responding: *"I tell you, not seven times, but seventy-seven times."* (verse 22). The King James version says, *"Until seventy times seven."* That is a whopping 490 times in one day!

Jesus did not mean we should keep a tally of the number of times a brother or sister wrongs us and whenever we reach seven or 490 in a day, we are then at liberty to withhold forgiveness. In fact, no one in their right mind would ever offend anyone seven times in one day, let alone 490 times. The underlying message is, we should not keep record of the wrongs done to us and we should forgive as often as needed. The point is, God's forgiveness toward us has no limit, and so should our forgiveness to others.

Here, we are being told that our acts of forgiveness toward our brothers and sisters should be unlimited. The Lord of your life demands unlimited forgiveness from you, not conditional forgiveness and certainly not "three strikes, I'm done" or the "once bitten, twice shy" attitude. Think! What if God takes that position toward you?

You may struggle to forgive the person who offends you the first time they wrong you, let alone seven times. This issue is not difficult for you only. I think Peter was either struggling with or needed clarity on this issue that is why he asked the question.

Therefore, after hearing this high call, this steep mandate to forgive their offenders, not once but as many times as needed, they immediate realized they cannot do it without faith in their Master, so they said to the Lord, *"Increase our faith."* (Luke 17:5). You must obey the same mandate today and like the apostles, you cannot do it without faith. It takes more than human willpower to forgive; it takes faith in Christ.

You must depend on God to obtain the strength and humility that are required to forgive those who hurt you. If the issue that lays heavily on your heart is due to harm that was done to you by the person you least expect looks like a mountain, or if it looks like something you cannot do, you are correct. You cannot do it, but the Christ who lives in you can do it.

Remember that faith moves mountains, including the mountains of pain, violation, infringement, betrayal, and offense. Activate the faith of Jesus Christ in you and watch the mountain melt like wax before you.

Your Response

Ask the Lord to increase your faith. **Refer** to Romans 10:17 where you can learn about the source of faith: faith comes through the message of Jesus Christ, and the message is heard through the Word. In other words, the source of faith is the Word of God. So, **apply yourself** to His Word and you will obtain the faith needed to forgive your offenders.

Day 32:
Be Ye Cleansed of All Filthiness of The Spirit

Get rid of all bitterness, rage and anger, brawling and slander, along with every form of malice. Be kind and compassionate to one another, forgiving each other, just as in Christ

God forgave you.

—Ephesians 4:31-32 (NIV)

It is one thing to be cleansed of the flesh, but it is quite another to be cleansed of the spirit. Usually, when a person thinks of getting clean, they think of the outer man or the physical man. They think of what can be seen with the naked eye, not the inner person. But in 2 Corinthians 7:1 (KJV), we are encouraged, as a matter of fact, we are commanded by our Father to *"cleanse ourselves from all filthiness of the flesh and spirit, perfecting holiness in the fear of God."* In 1 Peter 1:16, we are told to be holy because the God we serve is holy. And Hebrews 12:14 tells us that without holiness no one will see the Lord.

So let us now combine all three Scriptures: 2 Corinthians 7:1, 1 Peter 1:16, and Hebrews 12:14. To be holy, we must be clean inside and outside. Though we place emphasis on the outer man and too often ignore the inner man, by God's standards, we must be clean in both the inner and outer man. If the inner man — our spirit — is unclean, it will show through our deeds, which is the flesh / the outer man. When the Apostle Paul in 2 Corinthians 7:1 mentions the flesh, he is referring to our deeds, our conduct. So, the Apostle Paul is saying, our deeds, our conduct, our way of life must be in accordance with the character of Christ. And we must understand that our conduct (the flesh) will not be clean if our spirit is not clean.

It appears then, that to be holy, we must first cleanse our spirit, which would then result in the cleansing of our flesh. Holiness is a requirement of all followers of Christ. Why is that so? Why is holiness not negotiable? It is so because the God we serve is holy and He has no dealings with uncleanness. The requirement for holiness is further emphasized in Hebrews 12:14 where we are told that if we are not holy — if our spirit *and* flesh are not clean — we will not see God.

Impurities of the spirit can be things such as unforgiveness, bitterness, arrogance, anger, malice, wrath, envy, slander, rage, brawling, ungratefulness, and the list can go on and on. These impurities will not be in your spirit after being cleansed and sanctified by the washing of the Word (Ephesians 5:26; John 17:17). Instead, you will be kind and compassionate to others and you will forgive your offenders just as in Christ God has forgiven you. Your acts of kindness, compassion, and forgiveness will be demonstrated through your flesh (your deeds) because your spirit is clean.

Your Response

No one knows the condition of your heart but God. Not even you know the real state of your heart. Now, if you do not know the true state of your heart, you cannot fix it. Conversely, if only God knows the real condition of your heart, only He can fix it. Since you cannot do this yourself, it is best to **surrender** to God. **Ask** Him to create a clean heart in you and renew a right spirit in you. **Read** the Word of God, but not just with your physical eyes; **read** them with the eyes of your spirit. By doing so, the Word will wash and sanctify you.

Day 33:
Love One Another

> *34 "A new command I give you: Love one another. As I have loved you, so you must love one another. 35 By this everyone will know that you are my disciples, if you love one another."*
>
> *—John 13:34-35 (KJV)*

In this passage of Scripture, Jesus is talking specifically to those who have been with Him — the inner circle of His followers — throughout His earthly ministry. He is admonishing them to love one another (John 13:34-35). In many ways this is like the theme of church unity we see in the Gospel of John. We are to love our brothers and sisters in Christ. It is highly essential that we obey this command because this is how everyone (the world, our coworkers, and our unsaved relatives and friends) will know that we are disciples of Christ. This is how they will know we are true Christians. This act of loving others was a distinguishing mark of the followers of Christ then and it is no different today. In no uncertain terms, love — especially between fellow Believers — is meant to be the primary and most prominent sign of one's faith in Jesus Christ (John 13:35; 1 John 3:14).

Jesus did not say love those who agree with you or are kind and easy to love. There are brothers and sisters in Christ who are disagreeable, some are undeniably difficult to love. But the command remains the same — love one another.

Jesus commands us to love, but He does not leave us in doubt as to what that love should look like. He sets His own love for us as the standard to which all Believers should aspire. John 13 gives us a particularly intimate demonstration of the love Jesus had for His disciples. By Jesus taking the position of a servant and washing His disciples' feet, He gave them a demonstration of how they are to act towards one another (John 13:15). We are called to serve one another, to live with humility, and love in every situation. This is counter-cultural, but as followers of Jesus Christ, we are called to conduct ourselves in no other way.

It seems then that in imitating our Lord, in loving like He loves, we must forget about any sense of entitlement or right we think we have, or what we think we might deserve, but instead, we must tend to the needs of others. Jesus demonstrated His love for us best by laying down His life for us and He has commanded that we love one another as He has loved us. Jesus is pointing to the kind of love for a friend that would lead one to lay down their life for the friend. That is the kind of love that Jesus is commanding here: "*This is my commandment, that you love one another as I have loved you. Greater love has no-one than this, that someone lay down his life for his friends. You are my friends if you do what I command you.*" (John 15:12-14).

Jesus died self-sacrificially for us, and we too must be prepared to go to a comparable extent for our brothers and sisters in Christ. We do not need to die physically for our brothers and sisters in Christ to show we love them or to meet this command. But our pride, our right to defend ourselves, our need to have the last word, our need to explain ourselves and sometimes castigate people must die so that our brothers and sisters will experience our love.

Therefore, in cases of disagreement, love should make you keep silent, even if you are right. Love should make you speak words that foster peace and reconciliation. This applies whether you are victimized or not. The command does not change. Should you remain in a place or situation that perpetuates abuse and disrespect? Absolutely not! But in relationship with your brethren, your goal is to love, not to chide or argue, or defend, or accuse. Love in word and deed.

This commandment carries a very important element. Just by obeying this command, we tell the world that Jesus is love, and we demonstrate who we are. When we love others like Jesus commands, or when we lay down our lives for other Believers, including those who are disagreeable, we build them up and the world who is watching can come to know Who and what we know. We preach

Jesus when we love one another. My brothers and sisters, love one another in agreement and disagreement. It is the Lord's commandment!

Your Response

Read the love chapter — 1 Corinthians 13 — **list** all the attributes of love that is contained in the chapter. **Examine** yourself and **think** about how much you show love as defined by this chapter when in a dispute with anyone, especially a fellow Believer. Are you patient with your offender? Are kind to you offender although they are unkind to you? Do you dishonor your offender? Do you keep record of what they have done? **Pray** about these things.

Day 34:
Seek Peace and Pursue It

¹³ Keep thy tongue from evil, and thy lips from speaking guile. ¹⁴ Depart from evil, and do good; seek peace, and pursue it.

—*Psalm 34: 13-14 (KJV)*

One of the greatest benefit we enjoy as children of God is peace. Our God wants us to have inner peace and He wants us to live in peace with one another. When Jesus was on the cross and he said, *"it is finished."* (John 19:30, KJV), He was saying that the price for our salvation was fully paid.

Salvation entails being saved from sin and brought into relationship with Jesus Christ and with God our Father. This salvation is a comprehensive package, as it comes with peace, security, joy, grace, mercy, hope, love, and much more. However, while Jesus died for us to enjoy these benefits, we must do our part to enact them in our lives.

Psalm 34: 13-14 point to two (some may say three) ways we must behave to secure peace among Believers, unbelievers, and any mix of the two: control our tongue and the words we speak and do good, not evil.

The tongue *"is a fire, a world of evil among the parts of the body. It corrupts the whole body, sets the whole course of one's life on fire, and is itself set on fire by hell."* (James 3:6, NIV). James went on to say that *"All kinds of animals, birds, reptiles and sea creatures are being tamed and have been tamed by mankind, but no human being can tame the tongue. It is a restless evil, full of deadly poison."* (verses 7-8).

No wonder we had to get specific instructions to keep our tongue and watch over our mouths so that we do not speak evil words — words that are crafty and cunning or that stir up strife. A very important thing we ought to do when someone wrongs us is to ask the Lord to set a guard over our mouth and keep watch over the door of our lips (Psalm 141:3).

When we speak evil, it is because our hearts are drawn to what is evil and upon speaking evil, the next logical thing to do is engage in wicked deeds (Psalm 141:4). This is why the second way we must behave is to deviate from evil, and do good instead.

The tongue is a small element in the body, yet it can do great damage therefore we are instructed to keep our tongue from speaking evil and deceit. That is the first thing we must do to ensure there is peace. The need to ensure peace verifies that there must be some element of unrest or conflict, and in the context of interpersonal relationships, the most common cause of conflict is offense. Therefore, we are advised that when offended, we are to keep our tongue and not say anything that would exacerbate the situation.

In addition, we are advised to refrain from doing anything that is evil. We must not do anything that would harm the next person. No harm of any type — physical, spiritual, or emotional — should come t them due to our actions, and this command stands despite what the person did.

Your goal is to seek and pursue peace. Peace will not happen to you. Peace will not find you. You must take deliberate actions to obtain peace. You must do these things to secure and establish peace with your offender.

Your Response

Matthew 5:9 says, "Blessed are the peacemakers, for they will be called children of God." Peacemaking is your duty because you are a child of God. If you are argumentative, do not deny it. **Face** the truth and **take** correction from the Word. **Ask** the Father to give you self-control. Be prepared to be tested in this area, but get back up and press forward every time. Your Paraclete, the Holy Spirit will help you. Please know that this is an area you will grow in, and growth never occur in a single incident; it is a process. Let the Holy Spirit do the work in you.

Day 35: Slow Is Not Bad

[19] Wherefore, my beloved brethren, let every man be swift to hear, slow to speak, slow to wrath: [20] For the wrath of man worketh not the righteousness of God. [21] Wherefore lay apart all filthiness and superfluity of naughtiness, and receive with meekness the engrafted word, which is able to save your souls.

—James 1:19-21 (KJV)

When taken in context — which we should always do when seeking an understanding of the Scriptures — James 1:19-25 is speaking of the importance of listening to others (verse 19-21) so that we may foster healthy interpersonal relationships, but even more importantly, he is referring to the importance of listening to and receiving the Word (verses 22 to 25).

James was scolding a body of Believers who were speaking the Word more than they were obeying them. This is why he spoke as harshly as he did about the tongue. He is advising this body of Believers to be more willing to listen than to speak and upon hearing the Word, do what it says. The directive to listen before speaking is quite logical as one must first hear (know and understand) the Word before obeying the Word, and one must listen to what the other person is saying because speedy, unthoughtful responses precede wrath.

God can speak His Word in various ways, and He does. God's Words may come to our hearing from reading the Bible, from someone's teaching or preaching, or they may be spoken in casual conversations. It is a precious virtue to have the discipline to listen to those with whom we interact daily and under various circumstances. We should be quick to hear the Word of God in whatever form and through whatever avenue it comes. When we hear the Word of God with the ears of our heart, not just our physical ears, we will find that the natural response is to speak more thoughtfully and in a more timely manner. Just think what this practice would do to many of our relationships. Just think how many arguments and ongoing grudges would be nonexistent if this was our practice.

If we would listen more and talk less, especially when we are upset, there would be significantly fewer conflicts, and fewer people would be offended. We cause trouble when we speak before hearing what the other person is saying and before discerning what God wants us to say about the matter. We need to listen carefully both to people (James 1:19) and to God (James 1:22–25) before speaking. The Holy Spirit is always present to guide us into all truth. Our job is to listen and take heed.

When we listen before speaking, we will more likely respond appropriately, and will in turn mitigate impending conflicts. James said in verse 21 that if we listen carefully then speak, we would be clear of all offensiveness, all unpleasant behaviors, and malice. Interestingly, James suggests that listening to others — and not just listening to God — is how we rid ourselves of wickedness. So, it is clear here that while it is important to listen to God, we must listen to others. When addressing matters with others, move slowly. Listen, then speak.

When you are spoken to in a manner you do not like or are told things you would rather not hear — words of disagreement, criticism, dismissal, or otherwise — it is easy to respond hastily and in defense. But speaking out of turn engenders arguments, exacerbates conflicts, and fosters wrath. This type of behavior will only discredit your witness as a follower of Christ. It is much better to trust God to defend your position, rather than defend yourself by being angry or by speaking hastily. Untimely speaking produces anger, and anger does not produce God's righteousness. So, if you want to be in right standing with your Heavenly Father, be swift to hear and slow to speak. Slow in this case is not bad.

Your Response

Does your tongue often get ahead of your mind and heart? Do you find that you often regret what you say? Do you speak thoughtlessly and in anger? Do you gossip about or berate your offender? **Ask** the Lord to forgive you of the many thoughtless things you have spoken. **Tell** Him you are sorry for words you have spoken in anger or in gossip. **Ask** Him to help you sense when you are about to speak without thinking. **Ask** him to teach you how to check your heart before opening your mouth, even in the face of insults and offense. **Ask** Him to make you slow to speak. **Ask** Him to make you a person who is full of loving words, full of His Spirit, and overflowing with love, joy, peace, patience, kindness, gentleness, and self-control.

YOU CAN FORGIVE

Day 36: Forgiveness Demonstrated

Then said Jesus, Father, forgive them; for they know not what they do. And they parted

his raiment, and cast lots.

—Luke 23:34 (KJV)

A perfect demonstration of what forgiveness God's way should look like is the life and teachings of Jesus our Lord and Savior. After being brutally beaten, Jesus was hung on a cross. He could hear and see His abusers mocking and jeering Him. He was bleeding. His back was ripped open. His flesh, tissues, and muscles were hanging out from His body. The thorns from the crown that they sarcastically plaited pressed into His scalp, causing copious bleeding, the scalp being one of the most vascular areas of the body.

Jesus was unrecognizable from the brutal assault He had suffered, but even then, while on the cross, while being suffocated due to His inability to breathe freely, He prayed for His offenders. He said *"Father, forgive them; for they know not what they do."* (Luke 23:34, NIV). For the rest of us, this would be the opportune time to hate our abusers and to pray for the wrath of God to come upon them. Not many, if any of us would pray for the saving of their souls. But this is the standard to which God is calling us. Jesus is our example.

The crucifixion of Jesus was the most shocking spectacle of injustice. Hatred against God and the Savior of the world had reached the peak of humanities evil. We have and will never see or hear of another death as brutal and unjust as this one. Yet, it was then that we see the infinitely passionate love of God on display most. We see no hatred, revenge, or self-pity coming from Jesus. What we see is eternal forgiveness. Jesus demonstrated a depth of forgiveness that passes our understanding.

Despised, rejected, and dying on the cross, with outstretched arms of love, Jesus redeemed you, me, the entire human race from sin. This gives us a glimpse into the heart of the Father and His Son. If Jesus could love and pray for the very people who rendered Him — sinless though He was —to the most gruesome death that was set aside for criminals of the worst kind, we know He loves us, and we know He must be praying for us.

Jesus endured the agony of being crucified and the burden of sin for our salvation. Our loving Heavenly Father sent His son to die for our redemption from sin because He loves us. Likewise, God mandates that we forgive because He loves us. We know this truth because the forgiving of our offender is for our good. When we forgive our offender, it benefits us first.

Interestingly, this demonstration of forgiveness occurred in the worst situation possible. Could it be that the Father is telling us that forgiveness is never easy? Could it be that God is telling us that despite how egregious the situation, we must forgive? Could He be telling us that if Jesus could forgive in such a situation, we can do likewise in the bad situations that will never compare to what He endured?

We cannot respond affirmatively to this tall order to forgive without the help of the Holy Spirit. After Jesus paid the price for our salvation and ascended back to His Father, He sent the Holy Spirit — our Comforter, Teacher, Helper, and Guide — to live in us. So, we have the Holy Spirit to help us. And not only that, but Jesus is now seated at the right hand of God the Father, making intercession for us (Romans 8:34). Hebrews 7:25 tells us that He always lives to make intercession for us.

Regardless of the offense, God has mandated that we forgive. It is difficult to forgive our offender when we try to do so in our own strength. We need strength from the Holy Spirit to forgive. We should also take note that God has not asked us to do anything that He has not done and neither has He asked us to do anything that He will not empower us to do. Forgiveness was demonstrated by Jesus to show us that it is sacrificial and that it can be done, even in the face of injustice at its peak.

Your Response

Being like Jesus in thought, word, and conduct should be the deepest desire of any Believer. We see a characteristic of Jesus on display in Luke 23:34. He spoke life when He could have spoken death. He loved when He could have hated. **Pray** that the Shepherd of your soul will help you to be more like Jesus. **Pray** that the Holy Spirit will show you the hidden things in you that cause you to act contrary to the character of Christ.

Day 37: The Antidote for Unforgiveness

But I say unto you, Love your enemies, bless them that curse you, do good to them that hate you, and pray for them which despitefully

use you, and persecute you.

—Matthew 5:44 (KJV)

You are the one that has been wronged, but not only are you to comfort your offender, reaffirm your love for them, and do everything possible to live peacefully with them, you are also required to pray for them, bless them, and do good to them.

This is yet another indication that forgiveness God's way is indeed a high call. No one can do this in their own strength because naturally whenever a person is hurt by someone, they instinctively want to retaliate. But the God you serve, does not operate in the natural, He is all supernatural. And when you become a follower of Christ, you too must also operate in the supernatural. Without help from the Holy Spirit, which then enables you to act outside of the natural, you will never have the capacity to pray for, bless, and do good to your enemy.

Jesus taught that we show that we are God's children by loving those who do not love us. Loving those who love us is expected, but we show that the love of God is in us when we can love those who have done us harm. There might have been a time when someone was nice to you even though you had not been nice to them. How did that make you feel?

Kindness begets kindness, so when someone is nice to a person, that kindness usually elicit kindness in return. Therefore, our all-wise God has given us the recipe for peacemaking, and the ingredients of that recipe are to do good to our enemies and bless them, meaning speak well of them.

Jesus set the example for us to follow. He was rejected, humiliated, derided, and crucified. But while on the cross, He prayed for His enemies, saying *"Father, forgive them, for they do not know what they are doing."* (Luke 23:34, NIV). That is a demonstration of the kind of love and forgiveness that Jesus has and that He wants you and me to have for others — friends and enemies alike.

There is an adage that says, "You become intimate with the one for whom you pray, with whom you pray, and to whom you pray." Therefore, the command to pray for your enemy will only help to bridge the gap, it will repair any breach that offense has caused in a relationship.

I call Matthew 5:44 the full-proof remedy — the antidote — for unforgiveness. If you find it difficult to forgive your offender start by praying for them. Depend on the Holy Spirit, and let Him lead and direct you as you pray for them. Keep in mind that prayers for anyone will not be effective if not prayed out of compassion or in love. Your heart may not be bubbling over with love at the outset of praying for your enemies, but as you persist in prayer, trust me, God will fill your heart with love for them.

This is a doing of the Holy Spirit. Only Him can make you love your enemies, speak well of them, or do good to them, so depend solely on Him. As you pray for them, you will find changes taking place in your heart toward your enemies that are entirely out of your control and overtime your enemies will move from being enemies or offender to friend. God can and want to do this for you. Let Him do it.

Your Response

Ask your loving Father to help you follow the example that Jesus has set for you. **Ask** Him to help you love everyone, friends, and enemies alike, so that they will know that you are a true child of God. As the Holy Spirit directs you, **do** what He tells you to do. **Submit** to the Holy Spirit in the weakness of your flesh so that you can rise in the strength of the Spirit.

Day 38: Love the Lord With Your All

36 "Teacher, which is the greatest commandment in the Law?" 37 Jesus replied: "'Love the Lord your God with all your heart and with all your soul and with all your mind.' 38 This is the first and greatest commandment. 39 And the second is like it: 'Love your neighbor as yourself.' 40 All the Law and the Prophets hang on these two commandments."

—Matthew 22:36-40 (KJV)

Of all the commandments in the Bible, the greatest and most important is to *"Love the Lord your God with all your heart and with all your soul and with all your mind."* (Matthew 22:37). Man was made to worship God, but in the absence of love for God, our worship is unacceptable. In fact, we cannot sincerely or authentically worship anyone or anything unless we love the person or thing. Above everything else, God commands that we love Him, and not merely love Him, but we must love Him with everything in us: all our heart, all our soul, and all our mind.

Loving God is the first and greatest commandment (Matthew 22:38) and the second is like the first, which is to love our neighbor as ourselves (verse 39). Furthermore, all other commandments in the law depend on these two commands. Therefore, if we love God the right way, which is with all our heart, soul, and mind; if we love God with everything in us, that love will fuel and empower us to obey all other commands given by God.

This is why Jesus said *"If ye love me, keep my commandments."* (John 14:15). It is the love we have for God that will make us obey His commandments, and our love for Him is best demonstrated by our obedience to His commandments.

What Jesus meant by *"All the Law and the Prophets hang on these two commandments."* (Matthew 22:40) is, to obey all other commands given by God, we must first obey the first two commands, which are to love God with all our being and love our neighbor as much as we love ourselves.

Therefore, our love for God will make us love our neighbors, it will make us love our enemies, give to the poor, refrain from lying, refrain from sexual sins, and refrain from idolatry and everything else the Father has commanded us not to do.

Forgiveness is a command from the Father, and like other commands, it depends on the first two commands. Some see forgiveness as most difficult to do, but truthfully, if we love the Lord our God with all our heart, all our soul, and all our mind, we will be empowered to forgive, and forgiving our offenders will become easy, not in our strength but in the strength of the Lord.

Second to the first and greatest commandment is to love our neighbor as we love ourselves. Our neighbor is anyone other than us. There is no discrimination here. "Neighbor" includes our friends, extended family, children, spouse, enemy, offender, the homeless, the murderer, our pastors, our prayer partners, everyone. And Jesus further amplifies this command by warning that if we only love those who love us, there is no reward (Matthew 5:46).

So, the absolute best way to equip ourselves to forgive our offenders is to love God with everything in us. This will then empower us love our neighbor (includer those who hurt us) like we love ourselves. That means, if we want people to love us enough to forgive us when we hurt them, then we must love others enough to forgive them when they hurt us.

Your Response

THE SPOKEN WORD ON FORGIVENESS. A 40-DAY DEVOTIONAL

We live in a society that imposes a vast number of subtle distractions from God. You must **be alert** to the seemingly harmless things that dimmish your focus on and affection for God. These seemingly harmless things are called idols and God hates them. **Ask** the Lord to give you a love for Him that exceeds everything in your life. **Ask** Him to place in your heart a desire to please Him and to fill your mind with thoughts of His Love, so that you may grow in His wisdom and enjoy His peace through the love you share with your neighbors.

Day 39:
You Can Do It

I can do all this through him

who gives me strength.

—Philippians 4:13 (NIV)

Philippians 4:13 is one of the most broadly known New Testament verses, but it is also infamously misused. After telling his audience that he has experienced both poverty and affluence — he's been hungry and well-fed, he's been in need and he's been well off, and he's learned to be content, no matter what his circumstances are — the Apostle Paul writes these well-known words: "*I can do all this through him who gives me strength.*", meaning, if Jesus strengthened him to endure and be content in all these things, Jesus will do the same for him in any other possible situation.

The Apostle Paul is saying that no matter what your circumstances are, you can learn to be content. You can live to overcome it. No matter what your circumstances are, they do not have to kill you. How does he know? Because he has lived it and is now testifying about it. How did he live through these things? That is where verse 13 comes in. He lived through those circumstances only because Jesus gave him the strength to do so.

Verse 13 in the New International Version of the Bible says, "*I can do all <u>this</u> through Him who gives me strength.*", not "*I can do all <u>things</u> through Him who gives me strength.*" (emphasis added). The usage of the word "this" indicates that the Apostle Paul is referring to specific things, all the things he has been talking about, not "all things" in the sense that he can do anything he dreams of doing. The Apostle Paul is saying "I can do all things" is the ministry that God has sent him to do. He is saying that God can preserve Him through good and bad times, and that through the strength of Christ, he can persevere through anything.

The Apostle Paul did not make a broad stroke endorsement that God will support anything we set out to do and empower us to do whatever impossible things of which we can dream. The statement gives the assurance that we can do whatever God calls us to do, not whatever we decide to do. This is not a biblical exhortation you can apply to whatever goals you set for yourself. It is an encouragement that God can give you the strength to do whatever He has assigned to you, and He can give you the strength to obey any and every command He has dictated to you.

Like the Apostle Paul, you too have been called to ministry. To mention a few things, you are called to the ministry of reconciliation (2 Corinthians 5:18), you are called to let your light shine so bright that people are compelled to serve the God you serve (Matthew 5:16), and you are called to preach the gospel to all nations (Matthew 28:19). Those are some of the pleasant things to which you are called, but you are also called to endure hardship or suffering like a good soldier (2 Timothy 2:3), bear afflictions (Psalm 34:19), face trouble in this world (John 16:33), and deal with offenses when they come (Leviticus 19:18).

Like it was for the Apostle Paul, your walk with the Lord is not painless. You will face some difficult times, but your God is just and merciful. He did not set you up for failure. He will strengthen you through these things. He will strengthen you to forgive even your greatest offender. You can do it because His strength is available to you.

So yes, His has not commanded you to do anything that you cannot do. His grace is sufficient. In your weakness, He is made strong (2 Corinthians 12:9), and *"greater is he that is in you, than he that is in the world."* (1 John 4:4). If you have prepared a place of habitation in you for the Greater One, then without doubt, you can forgive.

Many have believed the lie of the enemy that because of the depth of the harm and injustice that was done to them, there is no way they can forgive their offender. This is a lie! Do not believe it! You can do it!

Your Response

Read James 4:7 in different translations of the Bible. **Pay close attention** to the word "submit." **Conduct further study** to get a full understanding of what James meant when he exhorted his audience to submit to God. Also, **read** John 14:26 and **take note** of the role of the Comforter. **Make a list** of what He has come to do in your life. Now **combine** the two verses and **pray** to the Father to help you to fully submit to Him so that the Comforter can work freely in your life.

Day 40: Abide in Him

I am the vine, ye are the branches: He that abideth in me, and I in him, the same bringeth forth much fruit: for without me ye can do nothing.

—John 15:5 (KJV)

In the natural, a branch that is broken off a tree cannot survive. Soon after being severed from the tree, the leaves will wither and dry up, the stem of the branch will dry up, and if there are fruit on the branch, they will rot. For the Believer, Jesus is the tree, and we are the branches. Like the natural tree, if we are not connected to the Tree — the True Vine — we will whiter up and die.

Jesus is pointing to the importance of remaining in fellowship with Him. In this verse, we have the assurance that we will produce fruit if we maintain fellowship with Him. Or said differently, if we stay connected to Jesus, we will produce fruit.

As followers of Jesus Christ, we cannot stay alive, neither can we bear fruit if we are not connected to and dependent on Jesus. Despite what the world and even some churches teach, we are not self-sufficient. We must admit our insufficiency to stay alive and bear fruit. We must totally depend on Jesus.

"*He that abideth in me, and I in him*" connotes fellowship and interaction between the two — Jesus and you. So, Jesus is inviting you into a dynamic relationship with Him. Apart from this, you will be fruitless, and not only that, but you will also die. There is no other option. You cannot produce fruit without dependence on Christ. You cannot produce fruit apart from fellowship with Him.

Fellowship with Jesus brings forth *much* fruit and allowing known sin in our lives breaks fellowship with Him? You do not want to be like the branches that are "in the vine," only in the sense that they are intertwined or touching the other branches. These branches are not truly part of the life of the plant. These are the people Jesus refers to as "in me" but barren (John 15:2). Those "branches" merely associate with Christian faith, identify with Believers, or attend a church. But only branches that are truly connected to the tree will produce fruit — just as only truly submitted and connected Christians will produce spiritual fruit (John 15:4).

You do not want to be "in" the Vine. Instead, you want to "abide in" the vine. You want to make a covenant relationship with Jesus Christ your dwelling place. This cannot be a place you visit when you are desperate, or a place you visit on special occasions, it must be where you dwell. Those who are "in" the Vine run the risk of hearing the Word but not obeying the Word (James 1:23). These are the individuals who see their shortcomings in the Word, but walk away and immediately forget what they saw (verse 24). Let this not be you.

You do not want to hear the message of forgiveness taught and preached and you do not obey the Word. You do not want to read about forgiveness and do not obey. You do not want to go to church week after week, but disobey God's Word.

You must abide in the Vine. You must realize that without Jesus, the True Vine, you can do nothing. Without being entirely dependent on Him, you will not have the will or the strength to forgive those who wrong you. So, because you want to bear much fruit, your response is to draw night to Him, knowing that when you do so, He will in turn draw nigh to you (James 4:8). Your response is to seek Him, because you know that when you do so, you will find Him (Jeremiah 29:13).

It is not possible to obey the Word of God without dependence on Christ. Neither you nor anyone else has the capacity to obey God in their own strength. You must abide in Him.

Your Response

THE SPOKEN WORD ON FORGIVENESS. A 40-DAY DEVOTIONAL

Pray this prayer with me: Dear Heavenly Father, I thank You for Your Word and I thank You for the Holy Spirit who has come to help me, teach me, and guide me into all truth; the truth of Your Word. Father, I need Your help to live a life of total dependence on You. I desire to have a dynamic fruitful relationship with You, but there are things in my life that are preventing me from rightly connecting with You. Please search and cleanse me of everything that is unlike You. Pursuant to reading and praying through this devotional, I want to walk in total obedience to You. I want to forgive my offenders and I want to love, bless, and pray for my enemies like You said I should. I do not want to merely "in" You, I want to "abide in" You. Father, thank You for hearing and answering my prayer, in Jesus precious name, amen.

Forgiveness Declarations

1. I choose life. I will forgive.
2. I choose to forgive others like Christ has forgiven me.
3. I will forgive God's way.
4. I will keep no record of what my enemies do to me. (! Corinthians 13:5)
5. I will love without discretion. I will love my friends, family, and enemies alike. (Matthew 5:46)
6. I will love, bless, and pray for my enemies. (Matthew 5:44)
7. I will diligently guard my heart against offense. (Proverbs 4:23)
8. I can do all things thru Christ. I can forgive! (Philippians 4:13)
9. I am kind and tender-hearted. I will forgive those who offended me just as Christ also forgave me of my sins (Ephesians 4:32)
10. I will be forgiven of my transgressions against others because I forgive others of their transgressions against me. (Matthew 6:12)
11. No iniquity will dwell in my heart, causing God to close His ears to my prayers. (Isaiah 59:2)
12. I release God's comfort and peace into the heart of those who have offended and hurt me. I pray for the Favor off God to come upon them and bless them in all their ways.
13. I do not judge as the world judge and neither do I condemn as the world condemns but I release those who have hurt and abused me into God's ever-loving arms. May they find peace and joy in their hearts forever more (Luke 6:37).
14. I will make every effort to live peacefully with all me. (Romans 12:18)
15. I will cover the deeds of my enemy with the love of working through me. (Proverbs 17:9)
16. I will submit to God so that I can get the strength I need to forgive those who hurt me. (James 4:7)

17. I will love the Lord with all my heart, all my soul, and all my mind so that forgiving my offenders will be easy. (Matthew 22:37)
18. The God of mercy who forgives us all my sins, strengthens me in all goodness, and the power of the Holy Spirit is my keeper.
19. Only Christ is in a position to condemn anyone. Christ died for me, Christ rose for me, Christ reigns in power for me, Christ intercedes for me. Therefore, I will not condemn but instead I will love my enemies. I will pray them and will bless them.
20. In Jesus Christ I am forgiven of every offense I have held against anyone. You bore my sins in Your body on the cross, that I might be dead to sin, and alive to all that is good. I declare in the name of Jesus Christ that I am forgiven!

Sources

1. Bible Exposition Commentary. https://versebyversecommentary.com
2. BibleRef. https://www.bibleref.com
3. Meaning and Commentary on Bible Verse, https://www.biblestudytools.com

> Please consider leaving an honest review of the book on Amazon or on Barnes & Noble.
>
> Thank you in advance.

About the Author

Dr. Rosemarie Downer is a dedicated follower of Christ who aspires to having the closest relationship with Christ possible. Her service in the body of Christ primarily involves teaching and preaching. She also spent well over 30 years serving in youth ministries. Other focus areas in her ministry include women and single adults. As well, she often ministers on issues that address emotional healing and well-being. She counts every opportunity to minister an ultimate privilege from God the Father and does not take it lightly.

She is the founder and former President of BRYDGES (Building Responsible Youth by Delivering Genuine Enrichment Services), over which she functioned as the President for 15 years – 2001 through 2016. BRYDGES provides enrichment services that address the emotional, educational, social, and spiritual needs of children and youths. She is a published author of The High Call of Forgiveness, It's A Mandate, The Self-Scarred Church, The COVID-19 Test: Church or God? Religion or Relationship? and several parenting handbooks. Additionally, she is the author of a comprehensive ministry development course – Find and Occupy Your Place and the Continuum of Care Youth Ministry Development Handbook.

Dr. Downer earned her doctorate degree in child psychology at the University of Maryland College Park in 1997. She served at The U.S. Department of Agriculture as a social science researcher for 20 years and as an adjunct professor at Bowie State University for 24 years. She is now retired from both positions and is currently a private consultant doing research and evaluation and doing what she dreamed of doing for years, and that is to write nonfiction books to edify the body of Christ.

The pivotal scripture verse for her ministry is 3John 2 – "Beloved, I wish above all things that thou mayest prosper and be in health, even as thy soul prospereth." Her most favorite Bible verse is Philippians 1:6: "Being confident of this very thing, that he which hath begun a good work in you will perform it until the day of Jesus Christ." Her favorite Bible character is Moses because he had the relationship with Abba Father that she so very deeply desires. Moses was able to talk to God the Father face-to-face and without riddle because of the close relationship he had with Him. That is her desire!

Other Books by the Author

The High Call of Forgiveness exposes the strategy of the enemy that has caused too many of us to believe it is too difficult to forgive. Undeniably, forgiving someone who has wronged us is difficult, but we can, if Christ lives in us. In the High Call of Forgiveness, Dr. Downer will take you on a faith journey by sharing the context of offense, why we hurt others, why it is as difficult for most of us to forgive, how we can forgive, how we can go beyond forgiveness to reconciliation, and how we can obtain emotional healing. She also gives permission to hurt but notes carefully that hurt must be addressed in a timely manner. This is an eye-opening and honest journey of self-examination. You will ask yourself and find answers to questions like: What got me here? How can I get past the pain? How is it that I love the Lord and know what the Word of God say about unforgiveness, yet I find it so difficult to obey? This book will change your life!

This **Leader Guide** is a companion to The High Call of Forgiveness. It provides the information needed to lead others into a deeper examination of the concepts discussed in the book and to look closely at scripture references that speak directly to the contents of the book.

The book, The High Call of Forgiveness exposes the strategy of the enemy that has deceived many into believing it is too difficult to forgive. Undeniably, forgiving someone who has wronged us is difficult. By going deeper into the concepts of the book, as a discussion leader, you will help many realize they can forgive.

The information covered in The High Call of Forgiveness and the accompanying Leader Guide will take the readers on a faith journey by examining the context of offense, why we hurt others, why it is as difficult for most of us to forgive, how we can forgive, how we can go beyond forgiveness to reconciliation, the costs of unforgiveness, the benefits of forgiveness, how we can obtain emotional healing, and more.

ROSEMARIE DOWNER, PH.D.

This **Student Workbook** is a companion to The High Call of Forgiveness. It's A Mandate. It provides the information needed for a deep examination of the concepts discussed in the book.

The book, The High Call of Forgiveness exposes the strategy of the enemy that has deceived many into believing it is too difficult to forgive. Undeniably, forgiving someone who has wronged us is difficult, but we can, if Christ lives in us.

Using the information covered in The High Call of Forgiveness and the accompanying workbook, you will take a faith journey by examining the context of offense, why we hurt others, why it is as difficult for most of us to forgive, how we can forgive, how we can go beyond forgiveness to reconciliation, the costs of unforgiveness, the benefits of forgiveness, how we can obtain emotional healing, and more.

Church or God? Religion or Relationship? is a rich resource for Believers as I challenge us to make God the head of our lives, to be in love with His heart, and to love and pursue His presence and not His presents. The book discusses how COVID-19 has forced us to worship outside of the physical building and how that has differentiated the boys from the men and the girls from the women in our walk with Christ. The book discusses how the blessings of today — good gifts from God — often distract us from God and dullen our appetite for Him. It details how we, God's beloved children, often unknowingly choose idols that pose as good things over our God who is superior, and it makes an appeal to followers of Jesus Christ to put God first. The urgent call in the book is to love God with all our heart, soul, and might, to even love Him (the Person Jesus Christ) more than good things such as ministry.

ROSEMARIE DOWNER, PH.D.

The Self-Scarred Church is a must-read for everyone, particularly pastors, church officers, and those aspiring to ministry. The Self-Scarred Church discusses the six most damaging self-inflicted wounds to the church — (1) Lack of Vision, (2) Survival Mentality, (3) Crab Syndrome, (4) Poverty Mentality, (5) Recognition Curse, and (6) King Leadership. Through an in-depth discussion of these six wounds, Dr. Downer, without reservation highlights the deficiencies and incompetence that for decades have slowed down and, in many ways, impeded the progress of the church. She uncovers some sleeping giants in the church but is careful to give some sound advice that are grounded in the Word. Church leadership — bishops, pastors, ministers, entire ministerial staff — and aspiring ministers and lay members of all Christian denominations should read this book.

Follow Me to Stay Connected

Facebook: BooksbyRosemarie & BooksbyRosemarieDowner

Instagram: books_by_rosemarie & books_by_rosemariedowner

Twitter: BooksRosemarie

Podcast: All Things Faith Walk

YouTube Channel: All Things Faith Walk

Email: info@booksbyrosemarie.com

Website: https://www.booksbyrosemarie.com

www.ingramcontent.com/pod-product-compliance
Lightning Source LLC
Chambersburg PA
CBHW032126090426
42743CB00007B/488